SpringerBriefs in Economics

For further volumes:
http://www.springer.com/series/8876

Carol Yeh-Yun Lin · Leif Edvinsson
Jeffrey Chen · Tord Beding

National Intellectual Capital and the Financial Crisis in Austria, Belgium, The Netherlands, and Switzerland

Springer

Carol Yeh-Yun Lin
Department of Business Administration
National Chengchi University
Taipei
Taiwan

Leif Edvinsson
Universal Networking Intellectual Capital
Norrtälje
Sweden

Jeffrey Chen
Accenture
Chicago, IL
USA

Tord Beding
TC-Growth AB
Karlstad
Sweden

ISSN 2191-5504 ISSN 2191-5512 (electronic)
ISBN 978-1-4614-8020-4 ISBN 978-1-4614-8021-1 (eBook)
DOI 10.1007/978-1-4614-8021-1
Springer New York Heidelberg Dordrecht London

Library of Congress Control Number: 2013940445

Printed on acid-free paper

Springer is part of Springer Science+Business Media (www.springer.com)

Foreword I

The economic crisis is a consequence of many parallel factors which are all related to globalization and digitalization. My main concern, assessing this in more detail from the European perspective, is that revolutionary global forces have not been taken early nor seriously enough by most national and regional decision makers. The Heads of European States and Governments have once again recalled the importance of fiscal consolidation, structural reform, and targeted investment to put Europe back on the path of smart, sustainable, and inclusive growth. The main question is how capable and ready are the national governments to tackling the complex and manifold issues of crises and to renewing even radically many of our public and private structures and processes.

The first basic requirement is that all the European Union Member States remain fully committed to taking the actions required at the national level to achieve the objectives of the Europe 2020 Strategy. The second basic requirement is that the national and regional governments, as well as people, are ready for radical changes. This booklet, and the other 11 booklets by the experienced authors, focus on National intellectual capital (NIC) and give necessary insights and facts for us the readers and especially for our in-depth systemic thinking of the interrelationships of NIC and economic recovery.

How should the national and regional decision makers tackle the existing knowledge of intangible capital? The focus needs to be more on the bottom-up approach stressing the developments on local and regional levels. I highlight our recent statements by the EU Committee of the Regions. The key priorities are to get more innovations out of research and to encourage mindset change towards open innovation.

The political decision makers are finally aware that the traditional indicators created for and used in industrial production cannot be applied to a knowledge-intensive, turbulent, and innovativeness-based global enterprise environment. Indicators that perceive the intangible dimensions of competitiveness—knowledge capital, innovation knowledge, and anticipation of the future—have been developed around the world, but their use has not yet become established in practice. This booklet accelerates the development and the use of these indicators.

This helps the local and regional, as well as central, governments in taking brave leaps forward on a practical level—giving greater ownership and involving all the stakeholders. This means the need of actions towards increasing the structural and relational capital of regions, both internally in communities of practice and in collaboration with others.

The new generation innovation activities are socially motivated, open, and collectively participated, complex and global by nature. The regions need to move towards open innovation, within a human-centered vision of partnerships between public and private sector actors, with universities playing a crucial role.

Regions should be encouraged to develop regional innovation platforms, which act as demand-based service centres and promote the use of international knowledge to implement the Europe 2020 Strategy, smart specialization and European partnerships according to the interests and needs of regions. For this to happen, we need to apply the new dynamic understanding of regional innovation ecosystems, in which companies, cities, and universities as well as other public and private sector actors (the "Triple Helix") learn to work together in new and creative ways to fully harness their innovative potential.

New innovative practices do not come about by themselves. One major potential is the use of public procurement. The renewing of the European wide rules must increase the strategic agility and activities of municipalities and other public operators as creators of new solutions. Especially, the execution of pre-commercial procurement should be reinforced even more in combination with open innovation to speed up the green knowledge society development, i.e., for common re-usable solutions in creating the infrastructures and services modern real-world innovation ecosystems are built upon. Conditions must be created that also allow for extensive development projects which address complex societal challenges and which take the form of risk-taking consortia.

One of our working instruments within the Committee of the Regions is the Europe 2020 Monitoring Platform, which broadly reviews and reflects the opinions and decisions on regional level all around Europe. It gives a flavor of cultural and other socioeconomic differences inside the EU. This brings an important perspective to the intellectual capital, namely the values and attitudes needed for citizens supporting policymakers on appropriate long-term investments and policies.

Emphasizing the importance of these issues, decision makers in all countries and regions worldwide need a deep and broad understanding of the critical success factors affecting the NIC. With all the facts and frames for thinking this booklet gives a valuable insight in today's challenges.

Markku Markkula
Advisor to the Aalto University Presidents
Member of the EU Committee of the Regions
Former Member of the Parliament of Finland

Foreword II

Financial crisis—words very much heard today. What is all this about, actually, and how to get a grip on what we experience today? The booklet gives an important insight on the factors affecting competitiveness and productivity in modern knowledge society. We need to see behind the obvious, and we need to have increasingly "qualified guesses" as the character of the society and industry has fundamentally changed.

What is very important to notice is the shift towards intangible value creation beyond the deterministic phenomena we saw very clearly in the industrial era. Cost drivers were the important ones throughout the industry. Mass production, bigger is better; very traditional productivity factors, was the mantra.

However, the production picture is changing. Increasingly value is created by the intangibles, often services related to the tangible components, and even totally in immaterial value creation, where perceptions and expectations determine the market value of the "extended product". We also see rapid change in organizational forms, we see new type of entrepreneurship growing besides the traditional industry clusters, we see smart specialization of regions and countries.

This means also that there will be clearly different and complementary roles of the actors in innovation and value creation ecosystems. Large companies, small ones and even microenterprises together with the public sector are traditionally seen as the active partners in such innovation environments. The real issue in the dynamic markets is, however, that the end users are increasingly to be taken on board as *active subjects* for innovation, and not merely treated as objects, customers. Markets need to be shaped and created in much more dynamic way than ever before. Open innovation beyond cross-licensing includes the societal capital as an important intangible engine for productivity growth. Innovation happens only when the offering is meeting the demand. Otherwise, we can only speak about inventions or ideas.

We need to have a close look at the intellectual capital and the different factors within it when we design our policy approaches. Short-term investments in process capital (infrastructures) and market capital seem to be very important for the manufacturing base as such, but at the same time measures for longer term intellectual capital development and efficiency need to be taken.

Increasingly, important is the *structure* and the open *processes* related to intangible capital and knowledge pools. For sustainable long-term development both the *human capital and renewal capital are crucial*, as they are directly related to the innovation capability of the region. The correlation between these factors and the GDP growth is undisputable. In knowledge intense industries talent is attracting talent, and the connectivity which modern ICT provides makes this talent pool fluid across disciplines, organizations, and geographical settings. It is imperative to modernize the innovation systems enabling the full dynamics needed for success in knowledge intense industries, beyond the traditional boundaries.

Measuring performance of innovation systems becomes increasingly complex due to the mash-up of different disciplines, having new types of actors and interactions between them. Hence, the importance of analysis of the various components of the national intellectual capital (NIC) (and equally on national innovation capability) as done in this booklet cannot be underestimated when making qualified guesses for operational choices to create functioning innovation ecosystems. The only predictable in true innovation is the unpredictability and the surprises. The role of the public sector is to drive strategy and measures enabling the unpredictable, and to catalyze a fluid, seamless and frictionless innovation system to grow, with strong interplay with the surrounding society.

We need to have courage to experiment, to prototype in real-world settings, to have all stakeholders involved to find and remove the friction points of innovation and to achieve sustainable innovation ecosystems for knowledge-intensive products and services.

I wish you interesting reading with this mind opening report.

Bror Salmelin
Advisor, Innovation Systems
European Commission
DG CONNECT

Foreword III

The 2008 global financial crisis hit the whole world with unprecedented speed, causing widespread financial panic. Consumer confidence dropped to the lowest level since the Great Depression. Taiwan, with an export-dependent economy, was seriously impacted by the crisis and the unemployment rate hiked while household consumption levels dropped. At the onset of the financial crisis, Prof. Lin was the Dean of Student Affairs here at National Chengchi University in Taipei, Taiwan. She was the dean in charge of financial aid and student loans and thus saw firsthand the direct impact the financial crisis had upon our students. The crisis was so devastating that Prof. Lin, along with the university, was compelled to launch several new initiatives to raise money and help students weather the difficult times.

I am very glad that she took this painful experience to heart and set herself upon the task of investigating the impact of the crisis; trying to look into the causes and consequences for policy implications, not only for Taiwan but for an array of 48 countries. In particular, she approaches the crisis from the perspective of "national intellectual capital (NIC)" which is very important in today's knowledge-driven economy.

Taiwan is an example of a knowledge economy and has enjoyed the fame of being referred to as a "high-tech island". Without an abundance of natural resources, Taiwan's hardworking and highly educated population is the single most precious resource that the island has. Acknowledging the value of such human resources and intellectual capital, we established the Taiwan Intellectual Capital Research Center (TICRC) under my leadership in 2003. Ever since then, Taiwan's government has continuously funded the university to conduct relevant research projects aimed at enhancing the intellectual capital of Taiwan. Having been thus endowed with the responsibility of nourishing future leaders in the public and private sectors, we have focused on building up our strength in innovation, entrepreneurship, and technology management related research and education.

To enhance intellectual capital research, we recently formed a joint team of professors for a 4-year project in order to leverage their respective research capabilities. Through this project we hope to provide policy suggestions for the government by exploring the creativity, innovation, and intellectual capital at national, regional, city, and county levels. The goal is to come up with an intangible assets (IA) agenda for Taiwan's future sustainability. Professor Lin is an integral member in this research team.

Following her 2011 book *National Intellectual Capital*: *A Comparison of 40 Countries*, this booklet series is Prof. Lin's second attempt at presenting her research, conducted under the sponsorship of TICRC, to international readers. As the Founding Director of TICRC and her President, I am honored to give a brief introduction of the value of this booklet series.

In comparison to her 2011 book, this series increased the number of countries studied to 48 and particularly focuses on the impact of intellectual capital on the 2008 global financial crisis. Rarely has an economic issue been systematically studied from the view point of IA, particularly at such a large scale of 48 countries. The research results show without a doubt that NIC is indeed an important economic development enhancer. In particular, the fact that countries with higher NIC experienced faster recoveries from the 2008 financial crisis provides a strong message for the policymakers.

In addition to providing insights to national policy, the booklet also summarizes the background of each country before the crisis, the key events during the crisis, economic development afterwards, and future prospects and challenges. Each volume affords readers a holistic picture of what happened in each country in an efficient manner. The linkage between NIC and this financial crisis also provides a different perspective of the crisis.

We are happy that Prof. Lin continues to share her valuable research results with international readers. I sincerely hope that her insights can garner more attention concerning the benefits of developing NIC for the well-being of every nation.

Se-Hwa Wu
Professor, Graduate Institute of Technology
and Innovation Management
President, National Chengchi University
Taipei, Taiwan

Preface I

There are "mounting risks of a breakup of the Euro zone." Such comments are frequent today on how the European leaders are handling the escalating crisis and its potential impact on non-European countries. But few leaders, reporters, or researchers are actually addressing the situation of national intellectual capital (NIC) and its signals. In addition to the financial crisis, is there an emerging NIC crisis as well? Why is it emerging? How should policymakers think about NIC? In what way does it need specific attention? When will the outcome and impact of taken NIC policy steps be realized?

In the midst of the European crisis, there are national interventions to address the issues mentioned above. In leading economical nations the investments going into intangibles now exceeds tangibles, and is positively correlated to income per capita. However, these still do not show up clearly in national mapping as well as policy making insights. Therefore, the New Club of Paris is focusing the knowledge agenda setting for countries on Societal Innovation (see www.new-club-of-paris.org).

Chairman Ben Bernanke of the U.S. Federal Reserve was addressing some of these same aspects in a key note speech in May 2011 hosted by Georgetown University: http://www.icapitaladvisors.com/2011/05/31/bernanke-on-intangible-capital/. OECD and the World Bank are developing NIC statistics, often based on the model from Corrado–Hultén. Japan has been developing both NIC and Intangible Assets (IA) at METI for some time now. Their research on IC/IA has resulted in a National IA Week with various key stakeholders, such as government agencies, universities, stock exchange, and enterprises. Japan is so far the only country in the world to hold such activities, and they have been doing so for the last 8 years. Australia, Singapore, South Korea, and China are currently undertaking various NIC initiatives. Other countries are also becoming more and more aware of NIC, with policy rhetoric centered on innovation, education, R&D, and trade. Despite this, the map for a more justified NIC navigation has been missing.

This booklet highlights NIC development for a number of countries, based on 48 different indicators, aggregated into four major NIC components of human capital, market capital, process capital, and renewal capital. The model here is a refined and verified statistical model in comparison to the Corrado–Hultén model. We call it the L–E–S model after the contributors Lin–Edvinsson–Stahle. Based on a deeper understanding and the timeline pattern it sets forth, this model will add to a better NIC navigation, not to mention knowledge agenda setting for countries.

Upon looking at a global cluster NIC map, it is evident that the top leading countries seem to be small countries, especially Singapore, the Nordic countries, Hong Kong, and Taiwan. For the U.S., Finland, and Sweden around 50 % or more of its economical growth is related to NIC aspects. Sweden, Finland, Switzerland, the U.S., Israel, and Denmark are strongly influenced in its GDP growth by focusing on Renewal Capital.

It might be that we will see a clearer map of the NIC ecosystem and drivers for wealth emerge in the extension of this ongoing unique research of NIC. This booklet will present a NIC map for various clusters of countries. It can be used for bench marking as well as bench learning for policy prototyping. The starting point is awareness and thinking of NIC, and its drivers for economic results. Based on this more refined navigation, NIC metrics can be presented.

Deeper understanding will emerge from this research, such as the scaling up of limited skilled human capital in one nation by using the globalized broadband technologies for migration and flow of knowledge (such as tele-medicine or mobile banking in Africa). This is also referred to as the IC multiplier. It might also be the way the old British Commonwealth was constructed, but without the IC taxonomy. In modern taxonomy it might be the shaping of NIC alliances for the migration and flow of IC between nations?

Another understanding that might emerge for policy making is the issue of employment versus unemployment. The critical understanding will be deployment of IC drivers. This will require another networked workforce of value networkers on a global scale, such as volunteering software and apps developers. However such volunteers do not show up in traditional statistics, for the mapping on behalf of policymakers.

On another level, there might be a clear gap analyses between nations to support the vision process of a nation. On a deeper level, it is also a leadership responsibility to address the gap of NIC positions versus potential positions. Such a gap is in fact a liability to the citizens, to be addressed in due time.

This will take us to the need for the continuous renewal of social systems. The so-called Arab Spring is explained by some as resulting from three drivers: lack of renewal of social systems, Internet, and soccer as cross class interaction space. The lack of social renewal and innovation is most likely critical early warning signals. For Greece, we can see such a tipping point occurred back in 1999.

On a global scale we might see that the concern for the Euro zone crisis should and can be explained by a deeper and supplementary understanding of NIC, in addition to financial capital. So we need to refine our NIC understanding, NIC mapping, NIC metrics, and NIC organizational constructs into societal innovation for the benefit of wealth creation of subsequent generations.

Leif Edvinsson
The World's First Professor of Intellectual Capital
Chairman and Co-founder of New Club of Paris

Preface II

Our first book *National Intellectual Capital: A Comparison of 40 Countries* was published in early 2011, at a time when the 2008 global financial crisis had been declared over yet the European region was still plagued with sovereign debt problems. Before we finalized the book, we were able to retrieve some of our raw data concerning the troubled countries, such as Greece, Iceland, Ireland, Portugal, and Spain. The results of our analysis based on data spanning 1995–2008 revealed some early warning signs of the financial turmoil in those countries. In my preface of that book, I mentioned the warning signs might reveal only the tip of an iceberg. At that time, my co-author, Prof. Edvinsson, and I decided to do a follow up study to trace the development of National Intellectual Capital (NIC) in as many countries as possible, particularly through the lens of the 2008 global financial crisis. This 12 booklet series is the result of that determination.

The 2008 global financial crisis came with unexpected speed and had such a wide-spread effect that surprised many countries far from the epicenter of the initial U.S. sub-prime financial problem, geographically and financially. According to reports, no country was immune from the impact of this financial crisis. Such development clearly signifies how closely connected the world has become and the importance of having a global interdependent view. By reporting what happened during 2005–2010 in 48 major countries throughout the world, this booklet series serves the purpose of uncovering national problems before the crisis, government coping strategies, stimulus plans, potential prospects, and challenges of each individual country, and the interdependence between countries. The 6 years of data allow us to compare NIC and economic development crossing before, during, and after the financial crisis. They are handy booklets for readers to have a quick yet overall view of countries of personal interest. The list of 48 countries in 11 clusters is provided in the appendix of each booklet.

Searching for financial crisis related literature for 48 countries is itself a very daunting task, not to mention summarizing and analyzing it. For financial crisis related literature, we mainly relied on the reports and statistics of certain world organizations, including OECD, World Bank, United Nations, International Monetary Fund (IMF), European Commission Office, the US Congressional Research Service, the U.S. Central Intelligence Agency, and International Labor Office (ILO). Some reliable research centers, such as the National Bureau of

Economic Research in the U.S., World Economic Forum, the Heritage Foundation in the U.S., and government websites from each country were also our sources of information. Due to the requirement of more update and comprehensive information, we were not able to use as much academic literature as we would have liked, because it generally covers a very specific topic with time lag and with research methods not easily comprehended by the general public. Therefore, we had to resort to some online news reports for more current information.

In the middle of 2012, the lasting financial troubles caused the European economy to tilt back into a recession, which also slowed down economic growth across the globe. However, almost 4 years have passed since the outbreak of the global financial crisis in late 2008; it is about time to reflect on what happened and the impact of the financial crisis. By comparing so many countries, we came to a preliminary conclusion that countries with faster recovery from the financial crisis have higher NIC than those with slower recovery. In other words, countries that rebounded fast from the crisis generally have solid NIC fundamentals, including human capital, market capital, process capital, and renewal capital. We also found that the higher the NIC, the higher the GDP per capita (ppp). This booklet series provides a different perspective to look beyond the traditional economic indicators for national development.

In an era when IA have become a key competitive advantage, investing in NIC development is investing in future national development and well-being.

Enjoy!

Carol Yeh-Yun Lin
Professor, Department of Business Administration
National Chengchi University, Taiwan
Taiwan Intellectual Capital Research Center (TICRC)

Executive Summary

Effectively assessing cross-border financial information through international cooperation facilitates the supervision of financial activities outside of the country.

One of the key factors of the financial crisis was that conventional financial systems failed to detect potential risks due to non-transparent information disclosure, including unsupervised financial activities across national borders. Our earlier national intellectual capital (NIC) research revealed warning signs of impending financial crisis for Greece, Iceland, and Ireland. Such findings indicate that NIC, albeit intangible, can provide valuable insights into risk control and strategy formulation. This booklet looks at the connections between the financial crisis and NIC development for Austria, Belgium, The Netherlands, and Switzerland.

Particularly, this report attempts to answer the following questions: How did these small European countries position themselves for long-term sustainability through building intangible NIC? What NIC pattern emerges for these countries? How did they weather through the 2008 global financial crisis for a fast recovery? What intangible assets will facilitate their future national development?

Data covering 2005–2010 for 48 countries indicate that *the higher the NIC, the higher the GDP per capita (ppp)*, accentuating the value of NIC as a driver in major countries/economics throughout the world. *For the 6-year average of NIC rankings among 48 countries, Austria ranks 11th, Belgium 19th, The Netherlands 10th, and Switzerland 2nd.*

The 2008 financial crisis caused severe impacts all across the globe and is considered to be the worst since the Great Depression of the 1930s. The crisis came with unexpected speed and spread into a global economic shock, which resulted in a number of bank failures. During this period, economies worldwide slowed, credits tightened, and international trade declined. In an effort to mitigate the crisis, governments and central banks across the globe responded with unprecedented fiscal stimuli, monetary policy expansions, and institutional bailouts. These measures had its desired impact and the financial crisis was declared over by the end of 2009.

However, the short global recovery in 2010 was overshadowed by the lingering sovereign debt problems in Europe, thus a global economic slowdown recurred in the second half of 2011. Despite the efforts of Euro leaders to prevent large economies like Italy and Spain from needing bailouts, Spain still asked for external financial assistance in June 2012. As of early 2013, economic recovery in most developed countries was still hampered by the weak global development.

The four European countries reported in this volume have relatively small domestic markets, with heavy dependencies on international trade. As a result, these countries were hard hit by the 2008 global financial crisis; yet, they all recovered faster than most EU countries. Their Global Competitiveness Index (GCI) ranking (Fig. 1.1) all advanced in 2011–2012, when compared to their pre-crisis level. Between 2005 and 2010, their *GDP growth* patterns were similar. However, Switzerland experienced early negative growth in 2008, yet it had a shallower decline in 2009 than the other three countries. In 2010, all GDP growth rebounded to an average of 1.5 %.

All the countries increased their general *government debt* after the financial crisis, except Switzerland. Belgium consistently had the highest government debt in this country cluster through the six years, reaching almost 97 % in 2010. Switzerland, with initial low debt of around 50 % of its GDP, managed to reduce its debt level year by year even during the financial crisis to around 39 % in 2010. The Netherlands had the most apparent debt rise after 2008, reflecting its financial stress during the financial crisis.

Aside from GDP growth and government debt, *unemployment* is another important indicator of the impact of the financial crisis. Over the six years all four countries had the lowest unemployment rates in 2008, reflecting the fact that they were not affected much right after the outbreak of the sub-prime crisis in the U.S. It was the aftereffects when global capital dried up and the sudden drop of international trade that really hit these countries. As a result, unemployment rates increased from 2009 onward, except for Austria in which the unemployment rate dropped in 2010. Belgium consistently had the highest unemployment rate amongst the four countries, averaging around 8 %. The other three countries were around 4–5 % over the years, lower than the 10 % EU average. For *consumer price inflation* (CPI), the hiked inflation in 2008 in each country was under control in 2009 and 2010. During the six years, Belgium had the highest CPI, The Netherlands had a relatively stable, and Switzerland consistently had the lowest CPI.

For NIC component capitals, over the studied six years (2005–2010), human capital (HC) did not vary much among the four countries. However, Belgium consistently had the lowest market capital (MC), process capital (PC), renewal capital (RC), and overall NIC of the four countries. On the contrary, The Netherlands had the highest MC from 2008 onward, Switzerland had the highest PC from 2006 onward, and Switzerland also had the highest RC and overall NIC through the six years. In particular, Switzerland ranked first in RC and fourth in PC and The Netherlands ranked fourth in MC among all 48 countries.

For the co-development of NIC-GDP, PC-GDP, and RC-GDP, Switzerland was consistently the best performer, followed by Austria and The Netherlands with intertwined development, and then Belgium bringing up the rear. For HC-GDP, Belgium had higher HC yet lower GDP per capita (ppp) than the other three countries. For MC-GDP, The Netherlands had higher MC than Switzerland with similar level of GDP per capita (ppp). Austria had the most apparent MC slide over the years.

For the *dynamic NIC ranking* changes in three time periods (2005–2006, 2007–2008, 2009–2010), the ranking gains represent increasing international competitiveness (among the 48 countries) after the financial crisis and vice versa. Austria lost its international competitiveness in MC on a relatively large scale of up to 10 ranks. Its PC also declined up to 6 ranks. Therefore, it is also important to look into the dynamic NIC international competitiveness over the years in addition to internal NIC national development.

The NIC 3D *trajectory analysis* was conducted to detect the enhancing and impeding factors of each country in reaching a targeted GDP per capita (ppp), benchmarking Singapore due to its high GDP per capita (ppp) (next to Norway only) and its high NIC (ranks 5) as well. To reach Singapore's GDP level, Austria has the longest distance (53.01 %) to cover, followed by Belgium (44.87 %), Switzerland (36.63 %), and The Netherlands (30.84 %) (see Table 3.4). Interestingly, even though Switzerland ranked number two in NIC development among 48 countries, its route to reach Singapore's GDP level requires a longer distance than The Netherlands with a NIC ranking of 10th. Raw data check reveals that Switzerland's exports and imports noticeably lagged behind that of The Netherlands. Austria having a longer distance than Belgium is mainly caused by Austria's low higher education enrollment, whereas Belgium has the best HC in this country cluster.

As of early 2013, the world economic recovery has been hampered by the pending debt problems in the Euro zone, the modest growth in the U.S., and the slowdown growth in Asia. The economies of these four small European countries were again affected and exhibited slower growth. Each economy's resilience to crisis will again be tested if the world plunges back into recession.

This economic crisis provides an ideal opportunity for nations to examine/renew/innovate the soundness of their economic system and the effectiveness of *national governance related to NIC*. The following implications are drawn from our research findings. Readers can refer to Chap. 5 for the rationale behind these implications.

1. Reducing government deficit through effective public spending and continuous structural reforms is the first priority in the wake of the financial crisis.
2. Government's swift and focused intervention of large banks is critical for stabilizing the financial markets, thus reducing the negative impact of the financial crisis.
3. Effectively assessing cross-border financial information through international cooperation facilitates the supervision of financial activities outside of the country.

4. High value added products and services in a niche market can mitigate the external impact.
5. Market diversification is important to reduce external impact for export-reliant countries.
6. NIC development goes together with the economic development and should be regarded as an enhancer of economic growth.
7. Detecting early warnings and designing country-specific strategy facilitate a more focused NIC development.

This report uncovers that Austria needs to pay more attention to its higher education enrollment and its international competitiveness in market capital. Belgium is running the risk of losing its competitive edge with lower NIC than its peers (except HC) in an era of knowledge economy. The Netherlands is relatively weak in long-term oriented human capital and renewal capital. Switzerland already has outstanding performance in both tangible GDP and intangible NIC; the area for further improvement is market capital.

In an era when the intangible asset has become a key competitive advantage, investing in NIC development is in essence investing in future economic development and well-being. NIC evolution should be nourished both from local culture viewpoint as well as global interconnectivity by social media. Based on the emerging new insights of values, societal history, as well as citizen relationships, a key focus for the future will be on the fusion of NIC and social service innovation as well as societal innovation, for the enabling of a new societal fabric.

Contents

List of Figures

List of Tables

Appendices

Abstract

In the first decade of the new millennium, the biggest event that caught worldwide attention was the 2008 global financial crisis, which was brought about primarily by ineffective governance, failed surveillance systems, and implementation flaws. These problems are mainly intangible in nature. Therefore, examining the financial crisis from the viewpoint of intangible asset provides a different perspective from traditional economic approaches.

National intellectual capital (NIC), mainly consisting of human capital, market capital, process capital, renewal capital, and financial capital, is a valuable intangible asset and a key source of national competitive advantage in today's knowledge economy. This booklet looks into the connections between the 2008 global financial crisis and NIC development with a special focus on Austria, Belgium, The Netherlands, and Switzerland.

In addition to the summaries of financial crisis impact, the aftermath, future prospects, and challenges of each individual country, NIC analysis based on data covering 2005–2010 for 48 countries reveal that the higher the NIC, the higher the GDP per capita (ppp). Graphical presentations of various types allow for intra-country and inter-country comparisons to position the reported four countries on a world map of NIC–GDP co-development.

By looking into tangible economic development along with intangible NIC development, this booklet provides valuable implications for policymakers.

Keywords Competitiveness · Economic policy · Financial capital · Human capital · Innovation · Intangible assets · Intellectual capital · Knowledge management · Research and development (R&D) · Science and technology policy

Chapter 1
Introduction

In late 2012, economic growth worldwide was slowing down. The growth in international trade has been disappointing, mostly due to a sharp decline in Euro zone imports. In emerging economies, such as China, India, and Brazil, production growth was also slowing down due to both a reduction in export and lower domestic spending (CPB 2012). For the United States, growth is expected to increase slightly to 2.25 % in 2012 and 2013. Global international trade is expected to recover to a certain extent in 2013.

The aftermath of the 2008 global financial crisis varied from country to country. Some have recovered from the turmoil and are picking up growth speed as in East Asia; some are still struggling to stand on their foot financially as Greece and Spain. Countries to be reported in this booklet showed recovery in 2010, yet their economies contracted again in the second half of 2011 due to lasting EU debt problems. In hindsight, it is valuable to reflect on what had happened during the last few years in different countries to gain some insights for future preventive actions.

Unexpectedly, what started off as sub-prime mortgage problems in the financial sector of the United States has snowballed into the deepest and most widespread financial and economic crisis in the last 80 years. With almost synchronized worldwide recession, global GDP was contracted for the first time since the World War II. Governments and central banks around the world have responded to the crisis through both conventional and unconventional fiscal and monetary measures in order to maintain financial order and help industries, private companies, and citizens wade through the difficulties.

The World Bank (2009) estimated that the 2008 global financial crisis would create an additional 53 million poor who live under US$2 per day, due mainly to the decline of the global economic growth. The magnitude of the crisis is so huge that it has disrupted the global financial system. Consequently, no economy in the world was completely isolated from the effect of the crisis. The greatest impact to the world economy was the downward spiral where the financial system problems caused companies to fail, household consumption and housing investment to slide, and unemployment to rise. The chain effect brought further decline for business

C. Y.-Y. Lin et al., *National Intellectual Capital and the Financial Crisis in Austria, Belgium, The Netherlands, and Switzerland*, SpringerBriefs in Economics,
DOI: 10.1007/978-1-4614-8021-1_1, © The Author(s) 2014

and industry along with increased losses on loans and financial investments at financial institutions.

In the wake of the crisis, causes of the disaster have become known. Briefly speaking, initially the collapse of sub-prime bonds in the U.S. resulted in a shortage in the global money market. As a result, huge amounts of foreign investments were withdrawn from invested countries all over the world to meet their headquarters' liquidity. Thus, the credit squeeze affected domestic market operations. Due to very negative cash flow, many companies slashed their production levels and cancelled or postponed investment projects (Mendonça 2010). With a tight money market, export demands dropped and unemployment increased. Adding to the scene is that some European Union countries were overlending and overspending even before 2008. Consequently, banks in many countries did not have enough money to support the repayment of foreign debts and corporate loans. Thus, confidence fell which directly hit the consumer market and global financial crisis set in.

One key factor that did not prevent the financial crisis from happening was that the conventional financial system failed to detect the potential troubles of sub-prime bonds, due to nontransparent information disclosure. Important data gaps are apparent, as the crisis has revealed a lack of sufficient granularity in data for monitoring financial sector developments (Enoch et al. 2011). Therefore, at the early stage of the crisis, management scholars criticized the inability of the traditional accounting system to reveal intangible assets that explain hidden values as well as risks for proper decision making (Reavis 2009).

In line with such criticism, intellectual capital (Edvinsson and Malone 1997) advocates the values of intangible assets and has gained increasing attention in today's keen global competition. After the financial crisis, the Chief Adviser at Tekes—the Finnish Funding Agency for Technology and Innovation particularly pointed out that "In the future, intangible assets, such as patents, advertising, education and training, are highlighted increasingly as a source of growth" (Palkamo 2011).

It is our deep belief that national intellectual capital, albeit intangible, can provide valuable insight to policy makers regarding future risk control and strategy formulation. Our book, *National Intellectual Capital: A Comparison of 40 Countries* (Lin and Edvinsson 2011; www.nic40.org), was born out of this belief and traces the national intellectual capital development of 40 countries over 14 years (1995–2008). The data analysis revealed certain warning signs of impending financial crisis for countries such as Greece, Iceland, and Ireland (Lin and Edvinsson 2011; 327–333). As a follow up study, this booklet series is an attempt to further explore the connections between the financial crisis and national intellectual capital (NIC) development.

The booklet series, in its entirety, will examine the national intellectual capital statuses of 48 countries from the period of 2005–2010 to glean new understanding about whether there is a NIC development pattern that distinguishes the fast recovery countries from the slow recovery ones. This is presented through a series of 11 country clusters, with each booklet focusing on one particular cluster.

The clusters are decided based upon several factors: Geographical proximity, similar size or similar phase of economic development. Focusing on one cluster at a time, we first probe within a single country, then extend to comparisons between multiple countries to see whether the situation before and after the crisis can be explained by the intangible national intellectual capital. Hopefully, this series will provide a different ex-post perspective when examining the financial crisis for future policy implications.

This volume, Volume Seven, will focus on four small European countries: Austria, Belgium, The Netherlands, and Switzerland. This booklet first provides an economic background to these four countries as a whole before going into each individual country's development individually. Through this process, the authors hope to paint a general picture of the economic condition and provide a basis for our dataset and analysis in future sections.

Chapter 2 briefly introduces the impact of 2008 financial crisis on the four countries. Chapter 3 elaborates the national intellectual capital development of these four countries. Chapter 4 describes issues beyond the financial crisis. And Chap. 5 concludes with future perspective and policy implications.

Economic Background

Since the economic history of these four countries goes back centuries, it is impossible to cover the entire spectrum in our work. As such, this background discussion will consider events in the relative recent history mainly from 2005 onwards that have the most direct impact upon the current economic conditions of each specific country. In addition, particular attention will be given to the 2008 financial crisis. In doing so, the authors hope that the background, in conjunction with our later data and analysis, will provide a "before, during, and after" picture of what was happening from a macroeconomic and intangible assets viewpoint.

In 2013, although some European Union countries are still trapped in the financial turmoil, these four small European countries have recovered from the 2008 financial crisis despite a little set back in the second half of 2011 due to lingering EU debt problems. To gain a general picture about their global competitiveness in the most recent year and before the financial crisis, we introduce hereunder the Global Competitiveness Index (GCI) published by the World Economic Forum. This index is relatively robust, for it takes into account the 12 distinct pillars[1] containing basic requirements, efficiency enhancers, and innovation factors that contribute to a nation's overall economic strength. Based upon commonly accepted economic theory, the development of a total 142 countries

[1] The 12 pillars include: institutions, infrastructure, macroeconomic environment, health and primary education, higher education and training, goods market efficiency, labor market efficiency, financial market development, technological readiness, market size, business sophistication, and innovation.

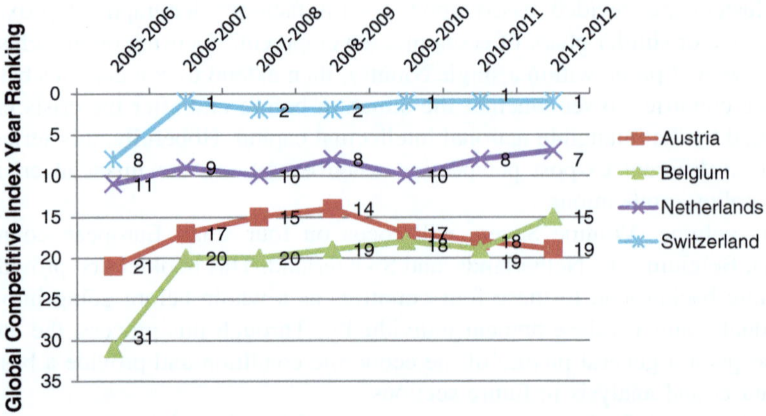

Fig. 1.1 GCI ranking of Austria, Belgium, The Netherlands, and Switzerland

was split into three stages in which different factors play a dominant role in determining the outcome of a country's economy. Stages 1, 2, and 3 are respectively characterized by being factor, efficiency, and innovation driven (Schwab 2011).

Plotting each country's annual ranking against a time series of seven periods, Fig. 1.1 displays a rough pictorial overview of the four countries' global competitiveness before and after the financial crisis. Over the years, all the four countries had GCI ranking improvement, especially with Belgium advanced its global competitiveness ranking from 31 to 15 and Switzerland from 8 to number one. Austria's GCI peaked in 2008–2009, yet declined after the financial crisis. Belgium's GCI remained stable during the financial crisis and advanced to 15 in 2011–2012. The Netherlands gradually advanced its GCI, even during and after the financial crisis. Switzerland has jumped from eighth place in 2005–2006 to first in 2006–2007 and then remained on a similar level before and after the financial crisis, which proves its economic resilience.

All four countries are export-oriented countries. Although export-led countries were hit more severely by this global financial crisis (Ragacs and Vondra 2009), only the GCI of Austria and The Netherlands showed the declining impact of the 2009 downturn.

According to Austrian National Bank (ONB 2012), the Austrian economy prevailed in a bleak international environment, ranked among Europe's growth engines in 2012 and is expected to remain so in 2013 and 2014. In June 2012, its economic projections have been revised upward for 2012 and 2013 due to the robust performance of the domestic economy, reflected in employment growth and pronounced investment cycle.

Belgium enjoyed a recovery following the global financial crisis. However, its newly formed six-party coalition government at the end of 2011 has to struggle not only to overcome ideological differences but also to fight against the mounting headwinds from the Euro zone (Market Research 2012). A particular concern is the national debt that is close to 100 % of its GDP, the impact of fiscal consolidation, and the Euro zone sovereign debt crisis. These issues left Belgium vulnerable to a deterioration in risk sentiment and slowdown in economic growth.

In 2013, the Dutch economy is expected to have a growth of 0.75 %, due to a slight improvement in international trade from 0.25 % in 2012 to 3.5 % in 2013; public finances will improve, mainly as a result of a restrictive fiscal policy, from a deficit of 4.5 % in 2011 to 2.7 % in 2013 (CPB 2012). However, The Netherlands is predicted to see growth resume only slowly, implying further increases in unemployment in the short term. In addition, its fiscal targets indicate a procyclical stance for the next couple of years (OECD 2012).

Switzerland has weathered the crisis relatively well, but not as well as previously thought. In 2012, Swiss GDP unexpectedly fell 0.1 % in the second quarter from the first quarter, due to the economy faltering as the Euro area's deepening slump and waning global growth erode export demand (Meier 2012). However, the economy rebounded strongly in the third quarter, mainly bolstered by stronger growth in government spending and inventory restocking (Focus 2012). Apparently, weak global economic activity and the perennial European debt crisis continue to weigh on the Swiss economy,

The next chapter will give a brief background and qualitative analysis of the 2008 global financial crisis as it relates to these four countries as a whole and individually.

Chapter 2
Impact of 2008 Global Financial Crisis

In order to present the impact of the 2008 global financial crisis, this chapter first describes the common problems in these four countries. Next, it graphically compares the GDP growth, total general government debt, unemployment rate, and consumer price inflation of the four economies during the time period from 2005 to 2010. Then, it elaborates on the financial impact on each country individually in the sequence of Austria, Belgium, The Netherlands, and Switzerland.

The first signs of the financial crisis appeared in the American financial system in the summer of 2007. Financial institutions in the United States had invested heavily in very risky assets with short-term debt securities, which resulted in rising default rates in the sub-prime mortgage market. Trust within the banking sector declined sharply and suddenly, leading to considerable problems in the market for interbank loans and severely undermined the mutual trust in financial institutions. The bankruptcy of Lehman Brothers in September 2008 triggered a further confidence crisis in the financial sector. Afterwards, interbank market rapidly dried up and a simultaneous increase in the price of trade credit led to a considerable decline in production and an unprecedented drop in world trade. With the high degree of international economic integration, national consolidation measures have dampening effects on trading partners' economies as well.

All these factors led to historically low confidence levels with world trade fell by almost 6 % quarter-on-quarter in the fourth quarter of 2008, and even by 11 % in the first quarter of 2009 (Masselink and Noord 2009). Unexpectedly, this rather specific housing bubble burst problem in the United States could grow into a global financial crisis, mainly because of the high degree of interconnectivity through investments in each other's products (Masselink and Noord 2009; Ragacs and Vondra 2009). This crisis was initially created by and in the financial markets, and then gradually spillover to the real economy through confidence fallout, capitals crunch, reducing consumption, and decreasing export demands. As a result, no country is immune from the impact of this financial crisis.

To drive Europe's recovery, in late 2008 the European Commission (Europa 2008) announced a comprehensive Recovery Plan based on two mutually reinforcing elements: first, short-term measures to boost demand, save jobs, and help

C. Y.-Y. Lin et al., *National Intellectual Capital and the Financial Crisis in Austria, Belgium, The Netherlands, and Switzerland*, SpringerBriefs in Economics,
DOI: 10.1007/978-1-4614-8021-1_2, © The Author(s) 2014

restore confidence; and second, longer-term "smart investment" to yield clean, energy-efficient higher growth and sustainable prosperity (Breuss et al. 2009). The Plan calls for a timely, targeted and temporary fiscal stimulus of around US$256 billion (€200 billion based on 11/26/08 exchange rate) or 1.5 % of EU GDP, within both national budgets (around US$217.6 billion or €170 billion, 1.2 % of GDP) and EU and European Investment Bank budgets (around US$38.4 billion or €30 billion, 0.3 % of GDP). In addition, to support small and medium-sized enterprises, the European Investment Bank (EIB) offers US$38.4 billion (€30 billion) in financing capital for the whole Europe until 2011 and the European Investment Fund (EIF) offers US$1.28 billion (€1 billion) Europe-wide as mezzanine capital (Breuss et al. 2009).With the monetary policy of the Euro system, liquidity was ample at all times, ensuring that financial markets would remain functional. In this respect, the Euro proved to be a protective shield for the Euro area countries (Fuentes et al. 2011). Based on Euro zone regulation, the guarantee on deposit accounts (current and savings accounts) was revised to US$133,905 (€100,000) (Government of The Netherlands n.d.). Yet, the backdrop as a Euro zone member is to relinquish national monetary policy autonomy.

These four relatively small west European countries are well-developed, open, yet have comparatively small economies. In general, they were in a better stance at the onset of the 2008 global financial crisis due to decade-long stable economic progress. However, with heavy reliance on exports, most of them were still hard hit by this crisis. The impact of the 2008 global financial crisis on each country can be easily observed from four graphs, namely the percentage of real GDP growth per capita, total general government debt percentage of GDP, unemployment rate of labor force, and consumer price inflation.

Comparisons of the Four Countries

This section presents four graphs in order to examine the four small European countries as a whole from 2005 to 2010. Figure 2.1 shows that all the countries had a relatively sharp real GDP decline in 2009, Switzerland also had negative growth (−0.10 %) in 2008. The decline in 2009 reflects the drastic impact of the financial crisis on these export-led countries. In 2010, all four countries had rebounded to a similar level of positive growth. Over the 6 years, Austria and The Netherland had similar patterns of the real GDP growth, while Belgium had a more flat growth before the financial crisis.

Figure 2.2 indicates that Austria had relatively stable government debt over the years with a little increase after the financial crisis. Belgium had the highest level of government debt, far exceeded the 60 % limit suggested by the EU even before the financial crisis. Its debt ratio rose a little after the financial crisis, reflecting the financial burden of its stimulus package. The Netherlands and Switzerland had similar and the lowest level of government debt to GDP among the four countries before the financial crisis. However from 2008 onward, the debt ratio of

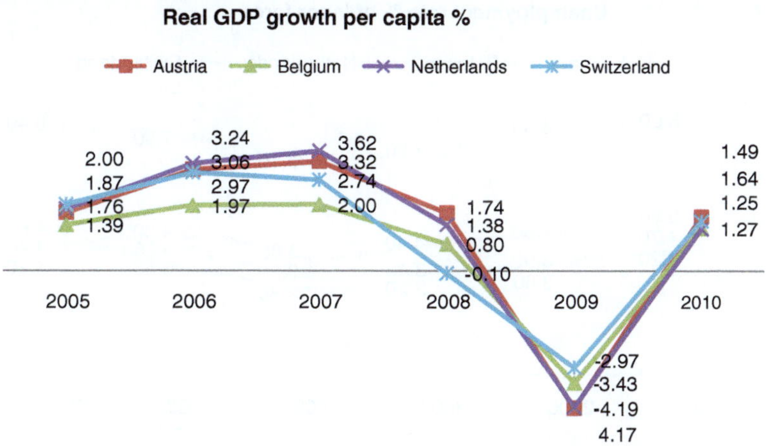

Fig. 2.1 Real GDP Growth per capita of Austria, Belgium, The Netherlands, and Switzerland from 2005 to 2010

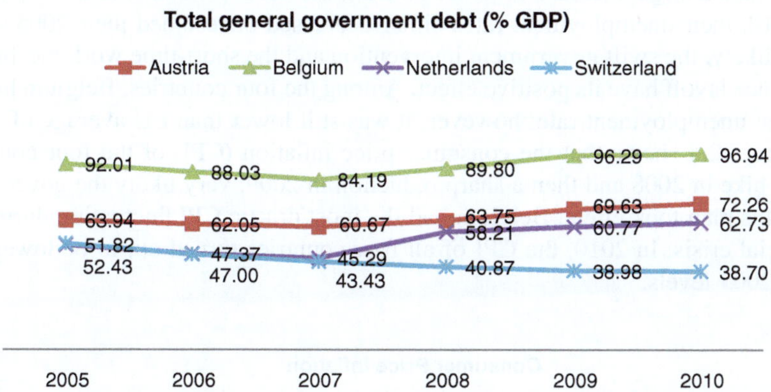

Fig. 2.2 Total general government debt (% GDP) of Austria, Belgium, The Netherlands, and Switzerland from 2005 to 2010

The Netherlands continuously increased, also reflecting the financial burden of its stimulus package. On the contrary, Switzerland managed to reduce its debt ratio even during and after the financial crisis. In general, The Netherlands had a sharper increase of government debt among the four countries.

Reinhart and Rogoff (2009) reported findings from their research on financial crises over the last 800 years that the aftermath of a financial crisis brings slow and halted growth, sustained high unemployment, and surging public debt—with the overhang of public and private debt being the most important impediment to a normal recovery from the recession.

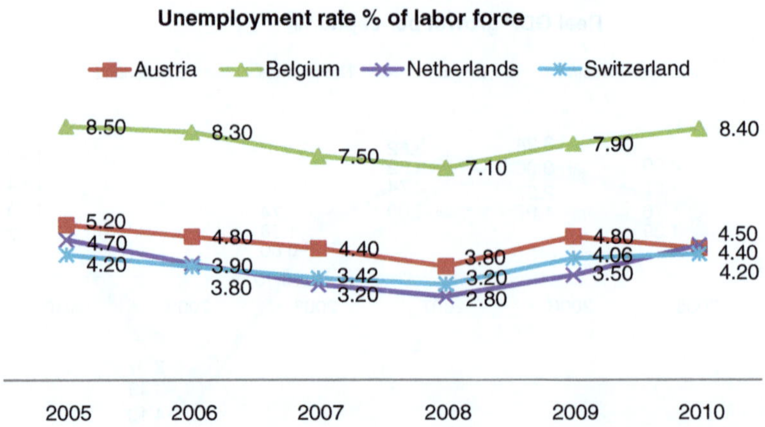

Fig. 2.3 Unemployment rate of Austria, Belgium, The Netherlands, and Switzerland from 2005 to 2010

Figure 2.3 shows that all the countries had an unemployment rate reduction in 2008, then a slight increase in 2009. Overall, the ratios remained relatively stable. In 2010, their unemployment rates either decreased or resumed their 2005 status. Very likely, the swift government intervention and the short-time work mechanism to reduce layoff have its positive effect. Among the four countries, Belgium had the highest unemployment rate; however, it was still lower than EU average of 10 %.

Figure 2.4 shows that the consumer price inflation (CPI) of the four countries had a hike in 2008 and then a sharp reduction in 2009; very likely the government stimulus plan took effect. Belgium had the most drastic CPI fluctuation during the financial crisis. In 2010, the CPI of all four countries turned out to be lower than their 2005 levels.

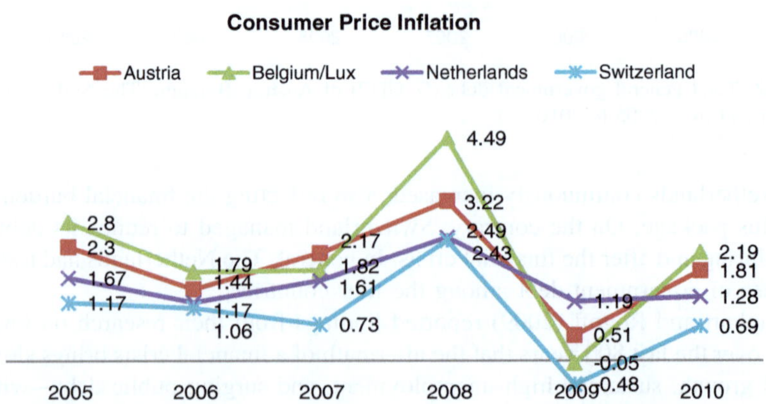

Fig. 2.4 Consumer price Inflation of austria, Belgium, The Netherlands, and Switzerland from 2005 to 2010

In general, the above four figures indicate that real GDP growth per capita and consumer price inflation of these four countries were clearly impacted by the 2008 global financial crisis. The total general government debt and unemployment rates do not vary too much before and after the financial crisis, except that The Netherlands had more obvious increase in government debt. In 2010, these four indicators largely return to their 2005 levels.

In what follows, we summarize the impact of 2008 global financial crisis on each individual country in the sequence of Austria, Belgium, The Netherlands, and Switzerland. The depth of the report depends upon the English literature available for each country. For readers to gain a general picture about the efforts that each economy has put into mitigating the negative impact of the financial crisis, we summarized the details of stimulus packages implemented by these four countries in Appendix 1. Please note that the reported package is based on publicly available data and is not an exhaustive list. In addition, the reported amount of stimulus package was based on the exchange rate at the time of each stimulus, and thus varies. Readers can also refer to Appendix 2 for the important meetings conducted by key global leaders during this financial crisis.

Austria

Austria is a well-developed, service-oriented (69.4 % of Austria's economy) market economy with close ties to other EU economies, especially Germany's (CIA 2012). Overall, machinery, steel, chemicals, electronics technology, and automobiles (especially engines and transmissions) are the most important export goods. In fact, Austrian goods and services export revenues were close to 60 % of its GDP prior to this financial crisis (Austrian Federal Economic Chamber 2011; OECD 2009a). In recent years, the Austrian real economy outperformed the Euro area average in relative terms, posting higher GDP growth, lower unemployment rates, improving international competitiveness, and growing current account surpluses. As a result, Austria was better positioned at the start of the financial crisis (Ragacs and Vondra 2009). Due to its increasing exports, the country was eventually also impacted by the external developments. However, the overall impact of this financial crisis on Austria has not been as severe as in other advanced economies (CIA 2012; Heritage 2011; OECD 2009a).

Before the financial crisis, Austrian banks had been very active across a broad spectrum of countries in the region, through cross-border loans and credits by subsidiaries. Particularly, Austrian banks' assets in central, eastern, and south-eastern Europe that were hit hard by the 2008 global financial crisis, as they reached over 60 % of the Austrian GDP (OECD 2009a). Unavoidably, Austrian financial institutions faced large losses with the economic downturn in those regions (CIA 2012). The financial sector uncertainties and the expectation of shrinking domestic employment subdued spending by households and enterprises. Austria thus experienced its deepest and most protracted recession since the mid-1950s.

In response, the Austrian government has reacted swiftly, taking measures in November 2008 to ensure the viability of the banking sector and to cushion the downturn through comprehensive and sizeable fiscal stimuli. Part of the federal government's stabilization program was the carrying-forward of income tax cuts into 2009, accompanied by two fiscal stimulus packages and a rescue package for the banking sector. The stimulus package totaled about 4.2 % of Austria's 2008 GDP with a dominating category of infrastructure investment, amounting to a share of around 75 % (Breuss et al. 2009). For growth projects of Austrian companies, a fund for medium-sized enterprises has been endowed with US$57.3 million (€40 million) each for 2009 and 2010 (Breuss et al. 2009). A series of monetary, financial, fiscal, and labor market policy measures have also been put in place since late 2008 to bolster banks' liquidity and capital together with the confidence of depositors and creditors (CIA 2012; OECD 2009a).

In addition to the monetary stimulus imparted by the Euro system, the Austrian authorities have introduced a US$130.9 billion (€100 billion) (36 % of GDP) package, including a top-up of the deposit guarantee scheme by US$13.1 billion (€10 billion), US$19.6 billion (€15 billion) for capital injections in financial institutions, and US$98.2 billion (€75 billion) for supporting interbank lending and for government guarantees of bank bond issuance (OECD 2009a). These measures have helped alleviate the strongest sources of tension in the financial system between October 2008 and April 2009 (OECD 2009a).

For fiscal policy, the automatic stabilizers played a particularly large role as the share of taxes and public spending in GDP was high, and social transfers were comprehensive in Austria. Moreover, discretionary stimulus was being injected, notably through measures to support households' purchasing power (including increases in family benefits, cancellation of student fees, and VAT cuts on medication), personal income tax cuts (brought forward from 2010 to 2009), and other measures such as new infrastructure investments (OECD 2009a).

Austrian labor market policies have protected the unemployed relatively well, initially through unemployment insurance and then through equally supportive social assistance. In this financial crisis, a rarely-used public subsidization scheme for enterprises that retained their employees despite drops in activity was expanded (OECD 2009a). The scheme was available for up to 18 months, and compensated income losses due to working time reductions of up to 90 % of the basic salary. Participating firms were encouraged to use the subsidized hours for requalification and retraining. By April 2009, 50,000 workers had been covered by this plan.

In hindsight, measures adopted by Austrian government aimed at securing financial stability appear broadly effective. As a result, Austria still registered real GDP growth of 1.7 % in 2008; yet, its GDP contracted 3.9 % in 2009 (CIA 2012; Ragacs and Vondra 2009). During the financial crisis, unemployment did not rise as steeply in Austria as elsewhere in Europe, partly because its government subsidized reduced working hour schemes to allow companies to retain employees. Consequently, the labor market in Austria has recovered quickly since the end of 2009 (Gurria 2011b).

Belgium

Belgium prospered in the past half century as a modern, technologically advanced European state and member of NATO and the EU. Tensions between the Dutch-speaking Flemings of the north and the French-speaking Walloons of the south have led in recent years to constitutional amendments granting these regions formal recognition and autonomy (CIA 2012). This open and private-enterprise-based economy has capitalized on its central geographic location, highly developed transport network, and diversified industrial and commercial base with services account for 75 % of economic activity (Heritage 2012). The Belgian economy was hit hard by the financial crisis, recording 3 % negative growth in 2009, forcing government intervention in major financial institutions (Fathallah 2010; IMF 2009). The Belgian stock exchange lost nearly 45 % of its value in 2008, depressing household assets by 15 % (IMF 2009). Belgium recorded a deficit of 6 % of its GDP in 2009, the highest deficit since 1993 (OECD 2011a). Job losses during this same year reached 23,300, raising the unemployment rate from 7 % in 2008 to 7.9 % in 2009. The crisis also sparked a deep recession in Belgium, in line with the rest of Europe (IMF 2009). The Belgian authorities' reaction to the crisis was prompt and generally effective (Fathallah 2010).

The financial sector in Belgium is large, internationally integrated, and dominated by conglomerates, with the four main banks holding 80 % of all banking assets (IMF 2009). The rapid expansion of some Belgian banks in emerging markets has been beneficial for both Belgium and host countries, but also has exposed them to increased risks. A particular concern is over its largest bank, Fortis, due to its costly and ill-timed acquisition of the Dutch operations of ABN-Amro in 2007. The purchase depleted Fortis' capital, while the credit turmoil made it difficult to obtain needed liquidity. As world financial conditions turned increasingly desperate, Belgian authorities were forced to step into three main Belgian-owned banks and a medium-sized insurance company during September–October 2008 to prevent a chain-reaction (Federal Planning Bureau 2011). As a result, more than US$24.6 billion was injected for bank recapitalization.

The bailouts include Fortis—the Federal government invested US$13.2 billion (€9.4 billion) to acquire virtually all its equity; Dexia—the Federal government and three regions together invested US$2.8 billion (€2 billion) in exchange for 11.5 % of its equity; KBC—the Federal government acquired US$4.9 billion (€3.5 billion) core capital and Flemish government has injected additional US$2.8 billion (€2 billion); and Ethias (insurance company)—the federal government, the Flemish, and Walloon regions each contributes US$0.7 billion (€0.5 billion) (IMF 2009). A state interbank financing was guaranteed and protection for savers was also improved by raising the guarantee for deposits to US$123,680 (Federal Planning Bureau 2011). The budget for 2009, together with a stimulus package announced in December 2008, provided a fiscal impulse of around 1 % of its GDP with a focus on reducing social contributions and boosting investment spending (IMF 2009). In addition, a whole series of measures were introduced aimed at reinforcing the purchasing power of social insured persons. Particularly, the increases in salaries and social benefits decided on prior to the crisis were not cancelled (Federal Planning Bureau 2011), which helped retain consumption and stabilize the economy.

At the federal level, the proposed measures included new and accelerated public investment, across-the-board reductions in social security contributions, a value added tax (VAT) reduction for selected construction activities, an increase in benefits for temporary unemployment, a limited subsidy for household electricity consumption, and steps to improve the liquidity position of the enterprise sector (IMF 2009). The federal government also invited the regions to each formulate its own set of measures, which turned out to be heavy emphasis on public investment in infrastructure and energy conservation, employment subsidies, and guarantee schemes to facilitate enterprise access to bank loans (IMF 2009). Particularly, there was a 1.5 % interest deduction for "green" loans for energy-saving investments (Meel 2009).

Like in the Euro area, economic activity in Belgium returned to positive growth in the third quarter of 2009. Mortgage applications have been on the rise since mid-2009, showing that the worst is already behind Belgium in the mortgage market. Data revealed that the upswing during the second half of 2009 continued in the first quarter of 2010 (Meel 2009). In general, Belgium weathered the crisis well with a relatively modest rise in unemployment. Subsequently, the economy had been recovering faster than the Euro area and the fiscal deficit was falling rapidly (Gurria 2011c).

The Netherlands

The Dutch economy is noted for stable industrial relations, moderate unemployment and inflation, a sizable current account surplus, and an important role as an European transportation hub. The country has been one of the leading European nations for attracting foreign direct investment and is one of the four largest investors in the U.S. (CIA 2012). After 26 years of uninterrupted economic growth, the small Netherlands' economy has become highly open and dependent on foreign trade and financial services. However, this export-led country with high bank exposure to U.S. mortgage-backed securities was hard hit by this global financial crisis (Enoch et al. 2011; CIA 2012).

2009 statistics indicated that Dutch export of goods and services amounted to about 80 % of its GDP, which is almost twice the European average; total foreign claims of Dutch banks amounted to over 300 % of its GDP; and the exposure of Dutch banks to the U.S. was 66 % of its GDP, the highest in Europe (Masselink and Noord 2009). Given this considerable importance of the external sector for the Dutch economy, unavoidably the economy is very sensitive to changes in world trade and the international financial market.

At the start of the crisis, the unemployment rate in The Netherlands was the lowest in Europe at around 3 % (Euro area average 10 %) and government debt in The Netherlands was low at around 45 % of GDP (Enoch et al. 2011; Masselink and Noord 2009). However, the negative effects of the financial crisis became more apparent in late 2008 and economic growth came to a grinding halt in the second quarter of 2009 (Masselink and Noord 2009). Fortunately, the relatively good starting position made it possible for the Dutch government to undertake massive operations in order to stabilize financial markets. In total, about US$126.2 billion (€90 billion) (15 % of GDP) was spent on rescue operations (Masselink and Noord 2009). Yet, its 2007 trade surplus of approximately US$47 billion was decreased to approximately US$43.2 billion in 2008 and US$42.2 billion in 2009 (U.S. Department of State 2012b). In 2008, the country's external current account surplus remained large (at 8.4 % of GDP, yet down from 9.8 % in 2007) (QFinance n.d.a) and GDP contracted 3.9 % in 2009, while exports declined nearly 25 % due to a sharp contraction in world demand (CIA 2012).

This global financial crisis still led The Netherlands into deep recession, despite a decisive government intervention to support the financial sector and a timely fiscal stimulus (OECD 2010). Particularly, the exposure of Dutch banks to hard hit Eastern European countries was at 11 % of its GDP, above the European average of 8 % (Masselink and Noord 2009). In addition, both Dutch households and corporations are relatively dependent on bank loans. In 2007, total indebtedness of households in The Netherlands amounted to approximately 120 % of its GDP, compared to 64 % in Germany, 49 % in France, and 47 % in Belgium (Masselink and Noord 2009). In 2007, bank loans to corporations amounted to 83 % of its GDP, compared to around 60 % of the GDP in Germany, France, and Belgium (Masselink and Noord 2009). The high dependence of The Netherlands on bank credit makes it relatively vulnerable to changes in the credit conditions.

In order to fight against the consequences of the crisis, the Dutch government launched three economic stimulus packages since November 2008. The first package was worth about US$8.3 billion, the second consisted mainly of government guarantees to stimulate lending and exports, and the third was worth US$9 billion, bringing the total value of the stimulus measures to US$17.3 billion, or approximately 2 % of GDP (U.S. Department of State 2012b). The state finances deteriorated further due to government interventions in the financial sector, including the nationalization of the Dutch activities of ABN-Amro/Fortis Bank (costing a total of US$37.6 billion), and capital injections to ING (US$12.5 billion total) (U.S. Department of State 2012b). The Dutch government also provided a cash injection of US$4.3 billion (€3 billion) to the insurer Aegon (QFinance n.d.a) and made US$286.7 billion (€200 billion) available for guarantees on bank loans (Government of The Netherlands n.d.; QFinance n.d.a). In 2009 and 2010, the government earmarked a total of almost US$8.6 billion (€6 billion) to stimulate the economy.

Based on OECD (2010), the measures were largely on the spending side and focused on four main pillars: maintaining employment (e.g., a reduced working time scheme, activation measures, retraining and job-search assistance, a debt assistance program for newly unemployed); shifting forward a number of planned public investment projects (monument restoration, costal works, waterway, road and bridge maintenance and construction works, health care centers, maintenance and construction of youth centers, schools, etc.); providing liquidity to companies (relaxation of rules on carrying over losses from 2008, broader R&D tax rebate, abolishing the air flight tax, energy investment tax credit, various tax cuts for SMEs, etc.); and supporting economic sustainability (investments in energy efficiency and a car scrapping scheme).

For The Netherlands, the third quarter of 2009 already showed a significant rebound in exports with 2.75 % quarter-on-quarter growth (Masselink and Noord 2009). The economy exited recession in mid-2009, as the effects of the fiscal stimulus, easier monetary policy, improved financial conditions, and an emerging recovery in world trade kicked in OECD (2010). Despite the large output contraction, the unemployment rate increased only marginally in 2009 (Enoch et al. 2011). The Netherlands recorded a deficit of 5.4 % in 2009 as a result of the crisis, increased government spending on stimulus packages, unemployment benefits, and financial sector bailouts (U.S. Department of State 2012b).

Switzerland

Switzerland is a peaceful, prosperous, and modern market economy with low unemployment, a highly skilled labor force, and a per capita GDP among the highest in the world (CIA 2012). Its economy benefits from a highly developed service sector and a manufacturing industry that specializes in high-technology and knowledge-based production. Although not an EU member, Switzerland has brought its economic practices largely into conformity with the EU's, in order to enhance their international competitiveness (CIA 2012). Over the last decade, macroeconomic stability and a highly developed and competitive financial sector reinforce Switzerland's position as a global financial hub (Heritage 2012).

As in most OECD countries, the global financial crisis pushed the Swiss economy into recession (CIA 2012; OECD 2009b), mainly because Switzerland's significant financial sector has exposed the Swiss economy to the global crisis. UBS is the largest bank in Switzerland, with total assets of over 400 % of Swiss 2007 GDP (OECD 2009b). Partly in connection with the U.S. sub-prime crisis, the financial crisis hit UBS hard—it had to write down US$53 billion of its securities holdings until mid-2009 (OECD 2009b). In addition, Swiss Re and Credit Suisse wrote down tens of billions of dollars in toxic assets as well. As a result, the Swiss National Bank (SNB) swiftly created the "StabFund" to acquire distressed assets, including a US$16.4 billion purchase of UBS' toxic assets in December 2008 (Qfinance n.d.b). The SNB during this period effectively implemented a zero-interest rate policy in a bid to boost the economy and prevent appreciation of the franc (CIA 2012). Still, the Swiss franc, traditionally reputed to be a safe haven among currencies in uncertain times, appreciated massively during the crisis

(Fuentes et al. 2011). The country's Swiss Market Index was dragged down by the banking sector's woes, ending down 33.5 % in 2008; in addition, the key metals, machinery, and electronics industry saw a sharp fall in new orders as well (Qfinance n.d.b).

However, despite the weight of financial intermediation in economic activity and significant losses of the large internationally active Swiss banks in the U.S. sub-prime mortgage market, Switzerland has performed better than most OECD economies during the financial crisis (OECD 2009b). The following eight key factors may explain Switzerland's resilience to the crisis (Fuentes et al. 2011; OECD 2009b).

First, Switzerland was in a comfortable fiscal policy position before the crisis hit, such as government debt ratio stood at only 46.5 % of GDP (Euro area: 66 % of GDP) in 2007, a stable labor market, and the absence of a real estate bubble preceding the crisis. Second, the swift and decisive government action played an important role to assure the stability of credit supply which mitigated the financial crisis impact. Third, economic policymakers made an important contribution to stability by reducing key interest rates, adopting economic stimulus packages, taking measures to stabilize the labor market and, above all, launching bank rescue packages to safeguard financial stability. Fourth, the SNB took unconventional measures to provide further stimulus, including exchange rate interventions due to the sizeable lending activity of Swiss banks in foreign currencies and continuous cooperation with other central banks on swap arrangements.

Fifth, labor market policy contributed to the resilience to the crisis, such as publicly funded short-time working schemes. In addition, the smooth integration of young job seekers into the labor force via the established vocational training system made a major contribution to stabilizing the labor markets as well. Sixth, Switzerland's sectoral and regional focus has supported the resilience of its foreign trade, thus the economic stability, leading to relatively unaffected domestic demand. Seventh, Switzerland's high degree of economic diversification is fairly resistant to cyclical fluctuations. Switzerland's export industry benefited from its regional diversification. In addition to 50 % of exports to the Euro area, Switzerland also conducts a substantial share of foreign trade with emerging countries, particularly with China, which experienced virtually no slackening of growth during the crisis. Eighth, Switzerland has taken global market leadership in the pharmaceutical industry and the manufacture of medical devices, which were affected relatively little by the crisis due to the low cyclicality of the generally state-run health care systems in the OECD countries. The pharmaceutical industry plus the manufacture of medical devices account for about 35 % of Swiss exports.

Switzerland is the first country to have emerged from the global financial crisis, as its crisis management efforts were rapid, systematic, and effective (Doerig 2009). Also because the Swiss got their monetary response right from the start, they had less need for a fiscal stimulus than other countries (Newsweek 2008). In addition, its financial sector has recovered swiftly from the global financial crisis (Heritage 2012). In general, the Swiss financial system has weathered the international financial crisis despite the severe losses of its two largest banks and one insurance company (OECD 2009b).

Chapter 3
National Intellectual Capital Development of the Four Small European Countries

In this chapter, we first present the development of national intellectual capital in these four relatively small European countries over 6 years, then graphically display the relationship between each individual capital with GDP per capita (ppp). Afterward, we describe the relative position of long-term and short-term intellectual capital and explain the dynamics of national intellectual capital for three time periods (2005–2006, 2007–2008, and 2009–2010). Finally, we illustrate the NIC trajectory of these four countries on three-dimensional (3D) 48-country landscapes.

National Intellectual Capital Development

The national intellectual capital measurement model used in this study is based on the indicators described in Appendix 3, containing human capital, market capital, process capital, renewal capital, and financial capital. This model has been statistically validated for its validity and reliability and the definitions of the indicators are listed in Appendix 4. This booklet series covers a total of 48 countries in 11 country clusters (see Appendix 5 for details).

For a full picture of all 48 countries being studied, Appendix 6 exhibits the scores and rankings of human capital, market capital, process capital, renewal capital, financial capital, and overall national intellectual capital (hereafter termed NIC) covered in this booklet series. Table 3.1 summarizes the status of the four small European countries compared to the total 48 countries reported in Appendix 6. Appendix 7 provides the individual country profiles with additional statistics. For the NIC ranking, Switzerland ranks 2 among the 48 countries, followed by The Netherlands at 10, Austria at 11, and Belgium at 19.

Among the five types of capital, Austria is comparatively better in process capital (ranked #8). Belgium is relatively better in human capital (#8), yet relatively weak in market capital (#23). The Netherlands is relatively better in market capital (#4). Switzerland has the best renewal capital (#1) among the 48 countries.

C. Y.-Y. Lin et al., *National Intellectual Capital and the Financial Crisis in Austria, Belgium, The Netherlands, and Switzerland*, SpringerBriefs in Economics, DOI: 10.1007/978-1-4614-8021-1_3, © The Author(s) 2014

Table 3.1 National intellectual capital scores and ranking of Austria, Belgium, The Netherlands, and Switzerland among 48 countries spanning 2005–2010

	Human capital		Market capital		Process capital		Renewal capital		Financial capital		NIC	
Country	Score	Ranking	Score	Ranking	Score	Ranking	Score	Ranking	Score	Ranking	Score	Ranking
Austria	7.229	14	6.203	11	6.982	8	5.296	12	9.708	10	35.418	11
Belgium	7.666	8	5.519	23	5.924	21	4.706	17	9.635	14	33.450	19
Netherlands	7.312	12	6.761	4	6.879	10	5.163	13	9.739	7	35.855	10
Switzerland	7.575	11	6.481	8	7.374	4	7.988	1	9.753	6	39.172	2

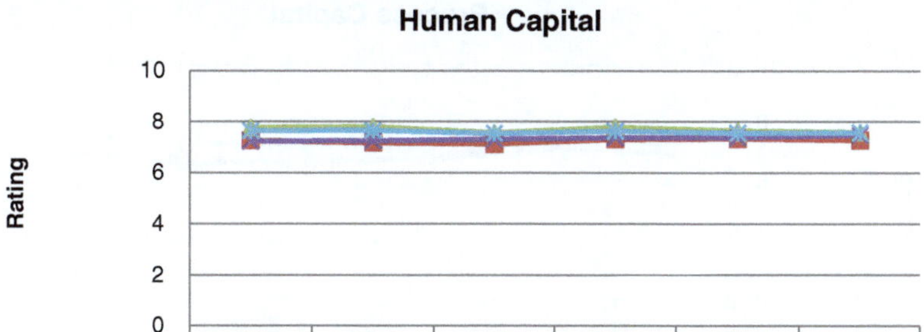

	2005	2006	2007	2008	2009	2010
Austria	7.25	7.16	7.10	7.29	7.31	7.26
Belgium	7.74	7.77	7.54	7.76	7.62	7.56
Netherlands	7.21	7.23	7.30	7.34	7.35	7.45
Switzerland	7.62	7.63	7.51	7.61	7.53	7.55

Fig. 3.1 Human capital of Austria, Belgium, The Netherlands, and Switzerland

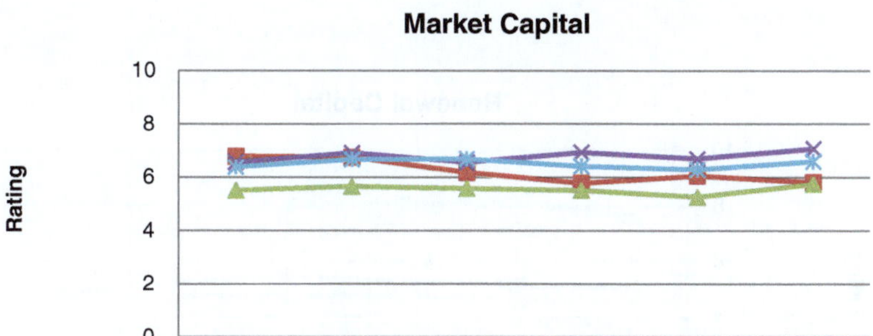

	2005	2006	2007	2008	2009	2010
Austria	6.76	6.72	6.15	5.76	6.03	5.79
Belgium	5.48	5.63	5.55	5.49	5.23	5.72
Netherlands	6.54	6.88	6.53	6.90	6.67	7.04
Switzerland	6.36	6.65	6.66	6.39	6.26	6.56

Fig. 3.2 Market capital of Austria, Belgium, The Netherlands, and Switzerland

Figures 3.1, 3.2, 3.3, 3.4, 3.5, and 3.6 compare human capital, market capital, process capital, renewal capital, financial capital, and overall NIC of the four countries, respectively. All the individual capital scores are based on a scale from 1 to 10 with the NIC score being the sum of the five capital scores.

Human Capital

National human capital mainly represents a nation's investment in nurturing qualified human resources, such as higher education enrollment, skilled labor, and

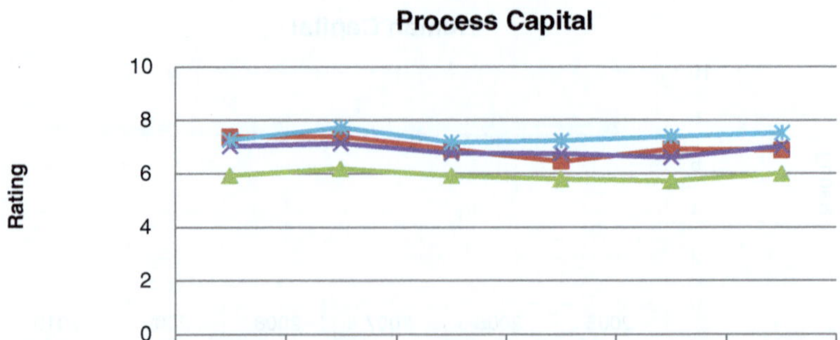

	2005	2006	2007	2008	2009	2010
Austria	7.38	7.38	6.89	6.45	6.91	6.88
Belgium	5.93	6.19	5.92	5.79	5.72	5.99
Netherlands	7.03	7.13	6.77	6.73	6.60	7.01
Switzerland	7.26	7.72	7.16	7.22	7.38	7.51

Fig. 3.3 Process capital of Austria, Belgium, The Netherlands, and Switzerland

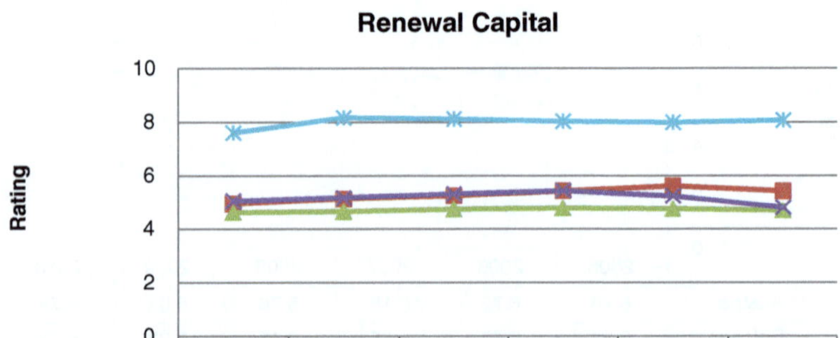

	2005	2006	2007	2008	2009	2010
Austria	4.94	5.12	5.24	5.43	5.62	5.43
Belgium	4.62	4.65	4.73	4.78	4.75	4.70
Netherlands	5.04	5.16	5.31	5.44	5.23	4.81
Switzerland	7.60	8.16	8.11	8.02	7.98	8.06

Fig. 3.4 Renewal capital of Austria, Belgium, The Netherlands, and Switzerland

public expenditure on education. It is a long-term oriented NIC (Lin and Edvinsson 2011: 323), taking time to develop yet not susceptible to external impact. Figure 3.1 shows that human capital of these four countries was relatively stable over the 6 years, with the scores close to each other. Comparing the score of 2010 and 2005, Austria and The Netherlands increase their human capital a little; whereas Belgium and Switzerland decrease a little.

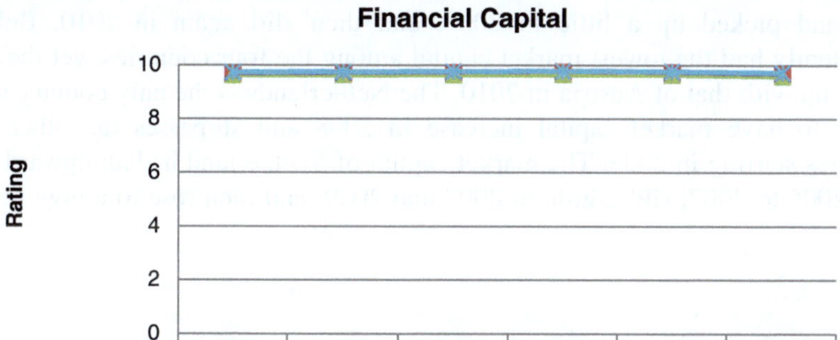

	2005	2006	2007	2008	2009	2010
Austria	9.69	9.70	9.72	9.74	9.72	9.68
Belgium	9.64	9.64	9.65	9.65	9.64	9.59
Netherlands	9.72	9.73	9.75	9.77	9.76	9.70
Switzerland	9.74	9.75	9.76	9.78	9.77	9.72

Fig. 3.5 Financial capital of Austria, Belgium, The Netherlands, and Switzerland

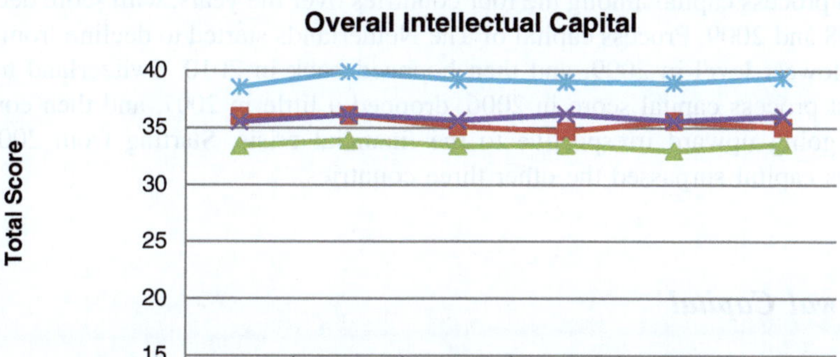

	2005	2006	2007	2008	2009	2010
Austria	36.01	36.09	35.10	34.68	35.60	35.03
Belgium	33.41	33.89	33.40	33.46	32.97	33.56
Netherlands	35.53	36.14	35.66	36.19	35.61	36.01
Switzerland	38.57	39.92	39.22	39.01	38.92	39.40

Fig. 3.6 NIC of Austria, Belgium, The Netherlands, and Switzerland

Market Capital

National market capital mainly represents international trade and relationship, such as cross-border ventures, globalization, and exports of goods. Figure 3.2 shows that all the countries had market capital increase comparing the score of 2010 and 2005, except Austria. The market capital score of Austria dropped in

2008 and picked up a little in 2009, and then slid again in 2010. Belgium consistently had the lowest market capital among the four countries, yet the score closed up with that of Austria in 2010. The Netherlands is the only country in this cluster to have market capital increase in 2008 and surpasses the other three countries starting in 2008. The market capital of Switzerland had an upward trend from 2005 to 2007, slid a little in 2008 and 2009, and then rose to a high level in 2010.

Process Capital

National process capital mainly represents the infrastructure required for building a prosperous society, such as capital availability, mobile phone subscribers, and government efficiency. Figure 3.3 shows that the process capital of these four countries was relatively stable over the 6 years, except Austria. Process capital of Austria started to decline from 2006 to its lowest level in 2008, yet bounced back in 2009, followed with a little decline again in 2010. Belgium consistently had the lowest process capital among the four countries over the years, with score decrease in 2008 and 2009. Process capital of The Netherlands started to decline from 2007 to its lowest level in 2009, and then bounced back in 2010. Switzerland had its highest process capital score in 2006, dropped a little in 2007, and then continuously going upward irrespective to the financial crisis. Starting from 2006, its process capital surpassed the other three countries.

Renewal Capital

National renewal capital mainly represents the capability of R&D and innovation, such as R&D spending, scientific articles, and patents. Figure 3.4 shows that renewal capitals of these four countries were relatively stable, except The Netherlands. Austria has a continuous score increase started from 2005 onwards until a little decrease in 2010. Belgium consistently had the lowest renewal capital score in this country cluster with a little decrease in 2009 and 2010. Renewal capital of The Netherlands progressed from 2005 to 2008, however decreased after 2009 onwards with a relatively larger scale than the other countries. Switzerland consistently had a relatively stable and the highest renewal capital score, far surpassing the other three countries.

Financial Capital

Financial capital is the GDP per capita (ppp) in US dollars converted to a score between 1 and 10. The score transformation process is explained in Appendix 3. Figure 3.5 shows the financial capital of the four countries on a 1–10 scale. The overlapping lines of this graph indicated that on a 1–10 scale, their financial capital is very similar. Yet in real dollars, the average GDP per capita (ppp) of 2005–2010 is US$37,738 for Austria, US$34,846 for Belgium, US$39,024 for The Netherlands, and US$39,621 for Switzerland. Switzerland has the highest GDP per capita adjusted by purchasing power parity.

NIC

NIC is the overall national intellectual capital containing the above five types of capital. Figure 3.6 presents the trends of NIC. Austria had a clear NIC dip in 2008. Belgium consistently had the lowest yet relatively stable NIC. The Netherlands had a clear NIC increase in 2008, yet decreased a little in 2009 and 2010. Switzerland consistently had the highest NIC, yet it had a three consecutive years decline started from 2007 and bounced back in 2010.

This figure shows that the intangible NIC remained relatively stable for countries with good quality human resource, well-developed infrastructure, and moderate level of renewal capability, even though there was disruptive external impact as this global financial crisis.

The Relationship Between Each Individual Capital and GDP Per Capita (ppp)

We investigate the relationship between each individual capital and economic growth by using Figs. 3.7, 3.8, 3.9, 3.10, 3.11, and 3.12. The graphs have four dimensions: the X axis changes from graph to graph (NIC, human capital, market capital, process capital, and renewal capital), the Y axis is a fixed dimension of GDP per capita (ppp) in US dollars (named GDP in brief hereinafter), the color shade represents renewal capital with red denoting higher levels of renewal capital, and the bubble size denoting the population of a nation. Figure 3.7 exhibits the relationship between NIC and GDP for all 48 countries. Figures 3.8, 3.9, 3.10, 3.11, and 3.12 display the co-development of the intellectual capital-GDP relationship over the 6-year timeframe for the four countries. Since financial capital is the 1–10 score converted from the GDP, there is no need to plot its relationship with GDP in US dollars. In the figures, 2005 is the starting point tagged with the name of the countries, and the ending point is 2010.

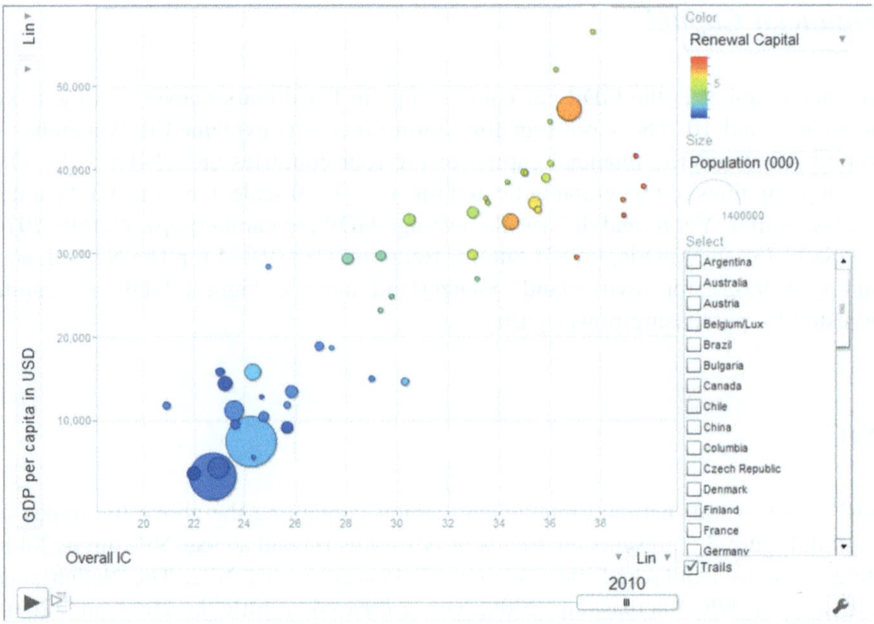

Fig. 3.7 NIC versus GDP per capita (ppp) for 48 countries in 2010

Figure 3.7 is particularly plotted to clearly show a full picture of the relationship between NIC and GDP for 48 countries in 2010. The strong positive correlation indicates that the higher the NIC the higher the GDP, and vice versa. Consequently, enhancing NIC is definitely a strategic issue that deserves the attention of national policy makers.

With the status of all 48 countries as the background, Figure 3.8 indicates that NIC and GDP co-development of the four small European countries falls at the upper right part of the 48-country continuum. Switzerland is at the top, followed by the intertwined development of Austria and The Netherlands. Austria's NIC declined over the years. Belgium is at the bottom among the four countries also with a backtracked NIC. Generally, the development paths of the four countries fall within the continuum, with Switzerland tilted to the X axis. Belgium has the shortest vertical path, representing its GDP growth over the years is in a smaller scale than that of the other three countries.

Figure 3.9 shows that the co-development of human capital and GDP of the four countries falls within the top range of the 48-country continuum. Again, Austria and The Netherlands have intertwined development. Belgium has the best human capital, followed by Switzerland. In this figure, the development paths are largely vertical, meaning there is not much human capital progress over the years, very likely due to an already high score in 2005.

The bubble formation of Fig. 3.10 is very different from that of other figures in this section in that it does not have a clear belt shape continuum from the bottom left

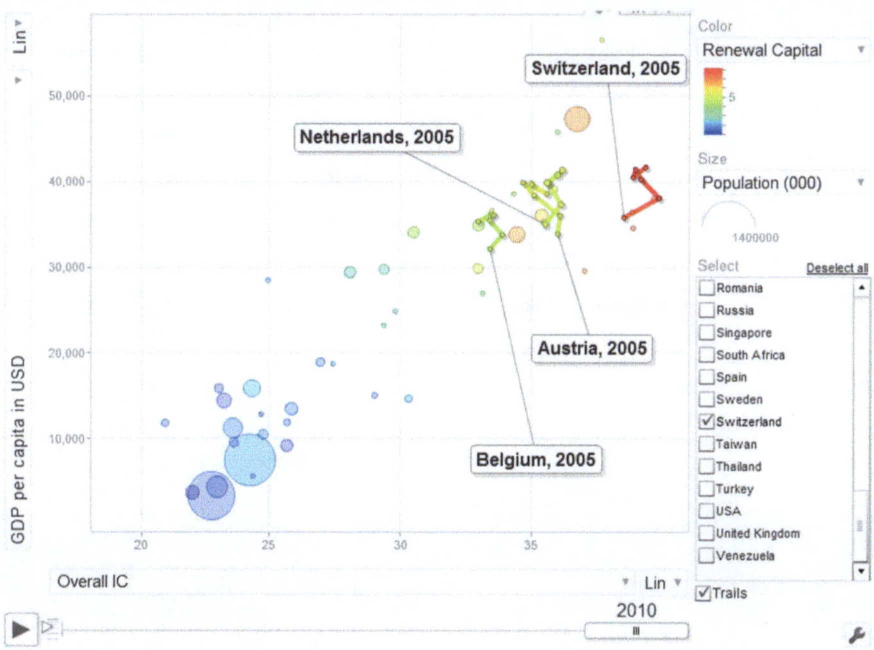

Fig. 3.8 The development of NIC and GDP per capita (ppp) for the four small European countries from 2005 to 2010

to the upper right. This means that market capital is not as highly correlated with GDP as the other capitals in this set of data. A further explanation is that market capital of advanced countries (generally positioned at the upper right) is not necessarily better than that of emerging countries. For instance, market capital of Belgium is lower than that of India (the second largest bubble at the bottom center). In 2010, The Netherlands has the highest market capital, followed by Switzerland, and then Austria sharing similar scores with Belgium (5.79 and 5.72). The market capital of Austria clearly decreased over the years; yet its GDP grew irrespective to this decline. A likely answer is that there are multiple sources of GDP growth which push up the GDP even though market capital was not an enhancer.

In Fig. 3.11, the belt shape continuum appears again, indicating that process capital is highly correlated with GDP in general. The development of the four countries is at the upper part of the continuum. For Austria and The Netherlands, their developments were again intertwined, with similar level of process capital explaining similar levels of GDP growth. Yet, process capital of Austria declined over the years. Switzerland was still at the top and Belgium at the bottom of the continuum. In 2010, process capital of Belgium resumed to its 2005 condition and Switzerland's advanced a little.

Figure 3.12 indicates that renewal capital and GDP co-development of the 48 countries had two formations. The spreading formation for the advanced countries is at the upper right, and the belt shape continuum for the less developed countries

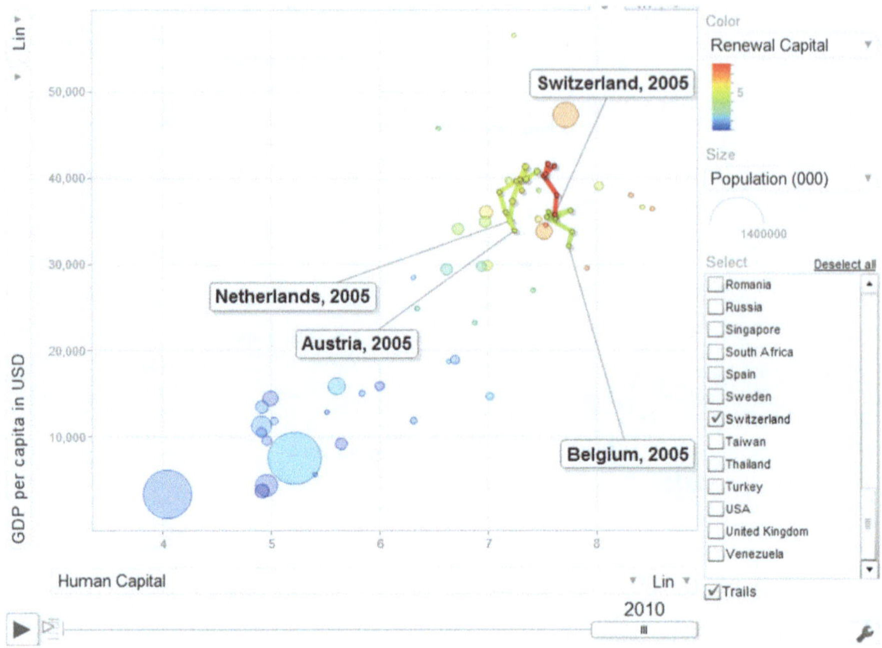

Fig. 3.9 The development of human capital and GDP per capita (ppp) for the four small European countries from 2005 to 2010

located at the bottom left. That means, for advanced countries, higher renewal capital does not necessarily go together with higher GDP and vice versa. Yet, for less developed countries, increases in renewal capital are accompanied with the higher GDP. From the formation of the bottom left continuum, it is clear that small increases in renewal capital were accompanied with relatively high GDP growth. This finding reveals a strong message that investing in renewal capital development may bring about GDP growth for less developed countries.

The renewal capital and GDP co-development of Austria, Belgium, and The Netherlands is at the middle upper range of the 48 countries. Again, the developments of Austria and The Netherlands were intertwined. Belgium's path is at the bottom among the four countries. Its vertical progression reveals Belgium has very little renewal capital improvement over the years. Switzerland's path is at the very top of the renewal capital, far apart from the other three countries.

Long-Term and Short-Term National Intellectual Capital

In addition to Figs. 3.9, 3.10, 3.11, and 3.12 that exhibit the relationship of each individual capital with GDP, Figs. 3.13, 3.14, 3.15, and 3.16 further plot the relationships between human capital and renewal capital, as well as between

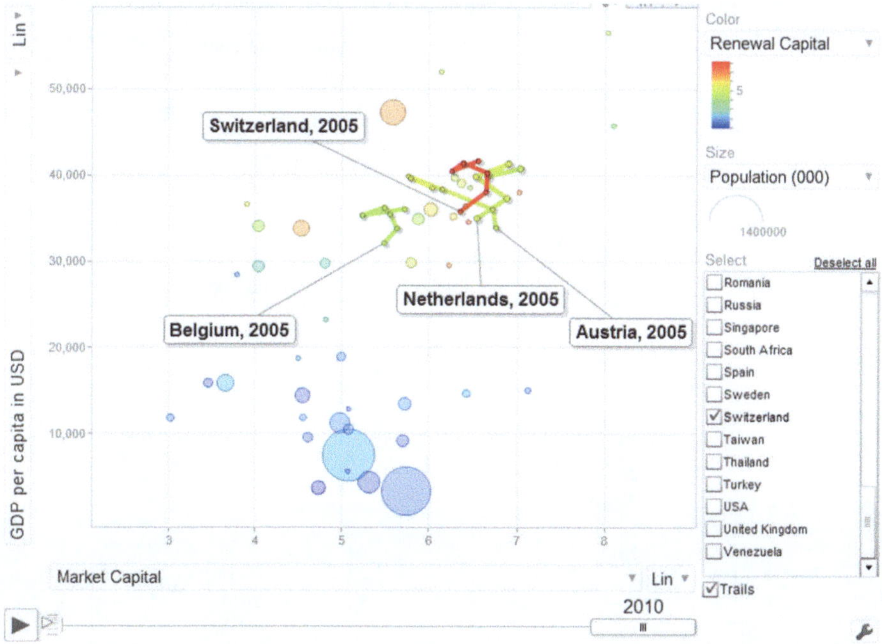

Fig. 3.10 The development of market capital and GDP per capita (ppp) for the four small European countries from 2005 to 2010

market capital and process capital. In our first study (Lin and Edvinsson 2011: 324), we found that the combined increase in human capital and renewal capital would lead to a nation's long-term development; whereas the combined increase in market capital and process capital might result in more immediate economic development. To present their relationships, Figs. 3.13 to 3.16 map the four capitals on a coordinate with two types of presentation. Based on the same data, Figs. 3.13 and 3.15 exhibit the scatterplot for the four countries only, whereas Figs. 3.14 and 3.16 show all the 48 countries as the background so that readers will know the relative positions of these four countries.

Figure 3.13 indicates that Austria and The Netherlands are at a similar level and intertwined with each other in their long-term NIC development, yet The Netherlands had higher human capital than Austria after the financial crisis (2009–2010). Belgium has high human capital yet low renewal capital. Switzerland's long-term NIC development is at the high–high corner of the scatterplot. Figure 3.14 shows a belt shape continuum tilted toward human capital axis. That is, generally speaking the 48 countries have better human capital than renewal capital, even though they are closely related. The figure indicates that Austria, Belgium, and The Netherlands are at the middle upper part of long-term NIC development among the 48 countries, which indicates there is room for further improvement. Switzerland surpassed all other countries in renewal capital and had

Fig. 3.11 The development of process capital and GDP per capita (ppp) for the four small European countries from 2005 to 2010

continuous improvement over the years. Yet, its human capital stood still before the financial crisis and declined a little after the financial crisis.

Figures 3.15 and 3.16 map market capital and process capital of the four countries on a coordinate. Market capital refers to the general assets embodied in a nation's relationship with international markets while process capital refers to the national infrastructure. For short-term competition, these are the two types of capital that can be expected to produce faster results if a nation is willing to engage in more extensive investments.

The two figures indicate that the short-term NIC development of these four countries is not too far apart from each other. Figure 3.15 shows a clear downward trend starting from 2006 for the countries in this cluster, except Switzerland with one year declining delay. All of them had a rebound starting from 2009, except Austria rebounded one year earlier, yet slid again in 2010. Austria especially had a larger scale of slide from 2006 than the other three countries. Generally speaking, even in these relatively wealthy and economically sound countries, the signs of trouble surfaced starting in 2006—much earlier than the outbreak of the global financial crisis in September 2008. Their short-term NIC recovery after the financial crisis (2009–2010) is in agreement with what had actually happened.

Figure 3.16 shows that, in a 48-country landscape, the market capital and process capital co-development of The Netherlands and Switzerland was at the

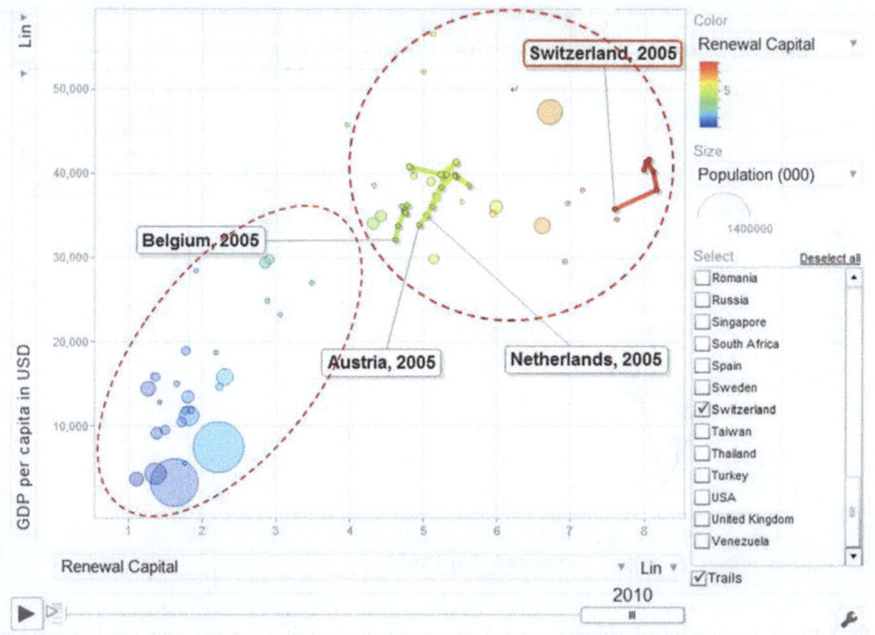

Fig. 3.12 The development of renewal capital and GDP per capita (ppp) for the four small European countries from 2005 to 2010

upper part of the continuum, Belgium at the middle upper part and Austria degraded to the middle upper part after the financial crisis.

Dynamics of National Intellectual Capital in Three Time Periods

The previous illustrations and graphs describe more internal progression or regression of NIC in each country with individual capital score changes over the 6 years and the path of development of various capitals. The ranking changes to be introduced in this section represent external competitiveness. Ranking, by and large, is a zero-sum game in which the advance of one country simultaneously marks the decline of another.

In order to probe the dynamics of NIC change before and after the financial crisis, we plotted Figs. 3.17, 3.18, 3.19, 3.20, 3.21, 3.22, 3.23, and 3.24 and Table 3.2 in three time periods: 2005–2006, 2007–2008, and 2009–2010. To have a clearer presentation, we separate the data in two sets. The first set contains capital scores and ranking changes of human capital, market capital, and process capital in Figs. 3.17, 3.19, 3.21, and 3.23. The second set exhibits capital scores and ranking changes of renewal capital, financial capital, and average NIC in Figs. 3.18, 3.20, 3.22, and 3.24.

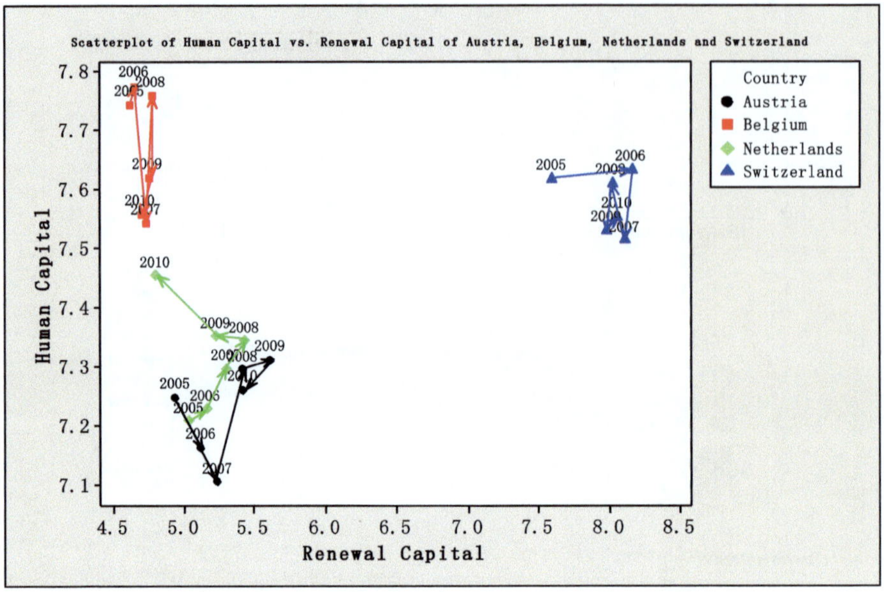

Fig. 3.13 A scatterplot of Human capital versus renewal capital for the four small European countries

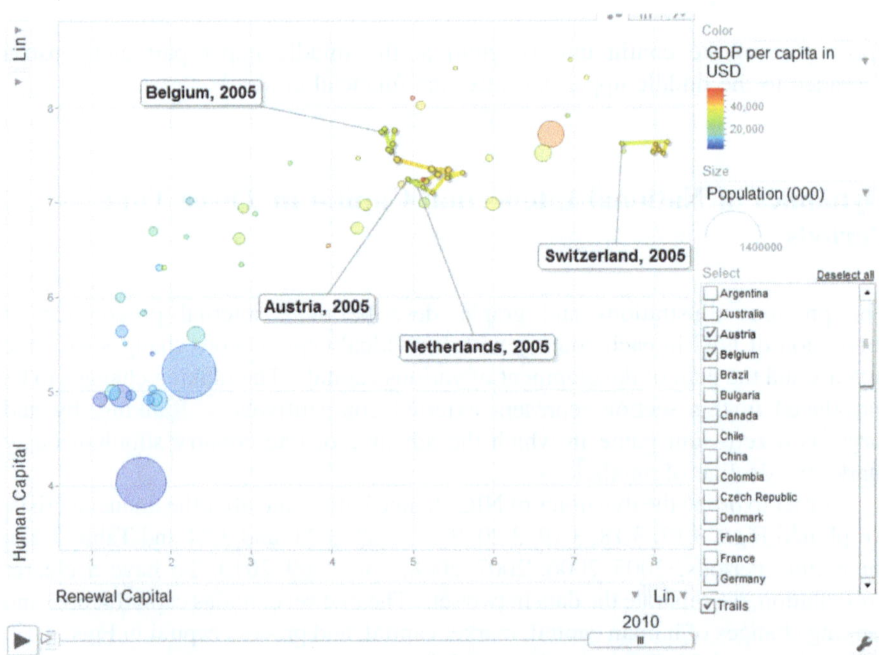

Fig. 3.14 Human capital versus renewal capital for the four small European countries

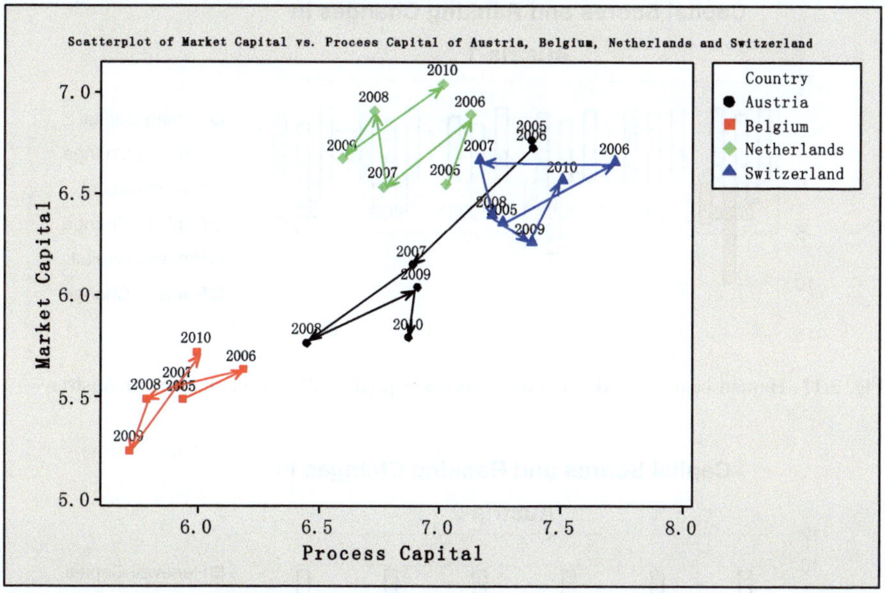

Fig. 3.15 A scatterplot of market capital versus process capital for the four small European countries

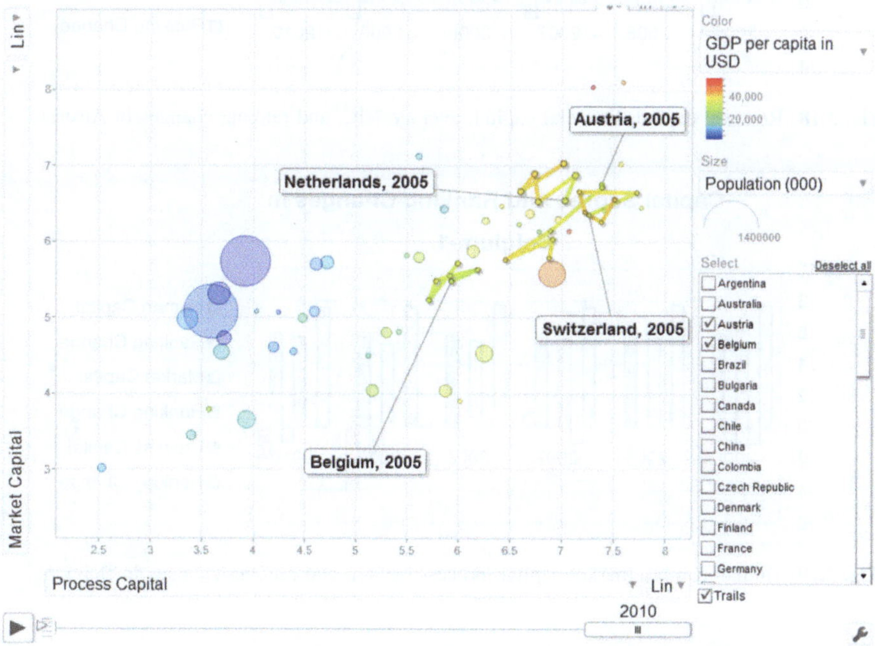

Fig. 3.16 Market capital versus process capital for the four small European countries

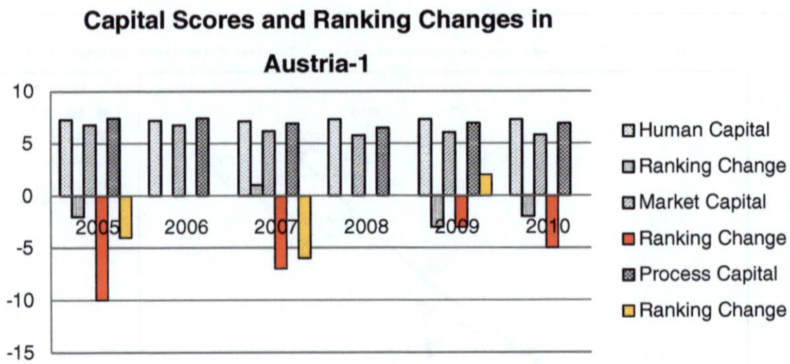

Fig. 3.17 Human capital, market capital, process capital, and ranking changes in Austria

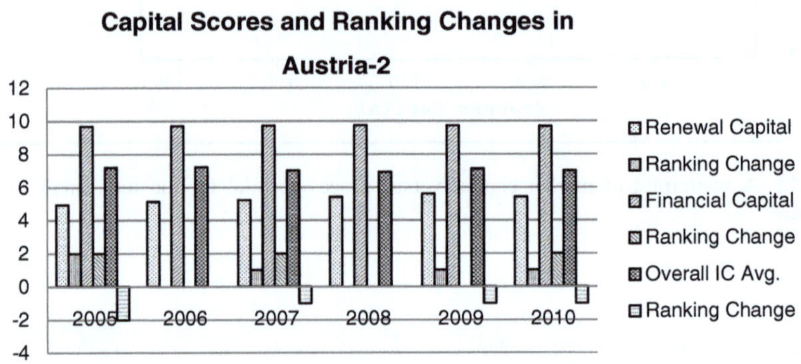

Fig. 3.18 Renewal capital, financial capital, average NIC, and ranking changes in Austria

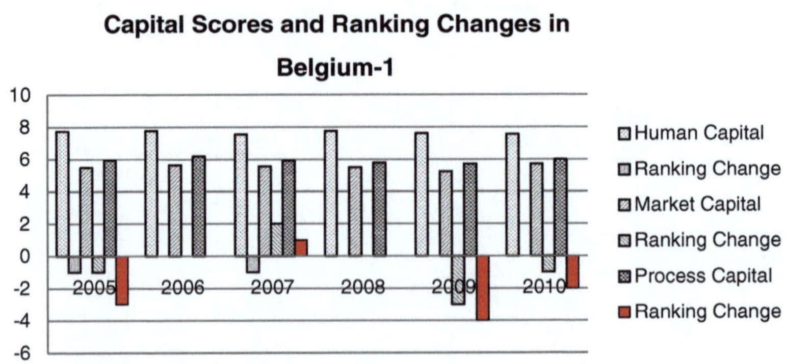

Fig. 3.19 Human capital, market capital, process capital, and ranking changes in Belgium

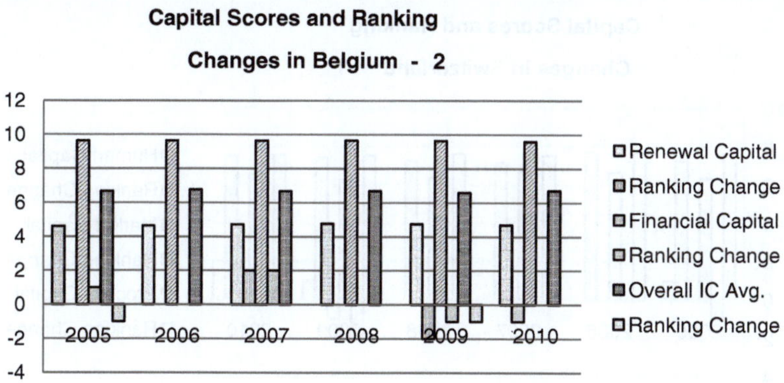

Fig. 3.20 Renewal capital, financial capital, average NIC, and ranking changes in Belgium

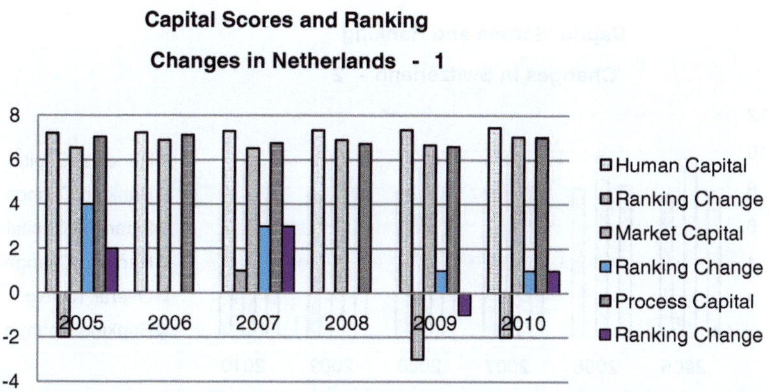

Fig. 3.21 Human capital, market capital, process capital, and ranking changes in The Netherlands

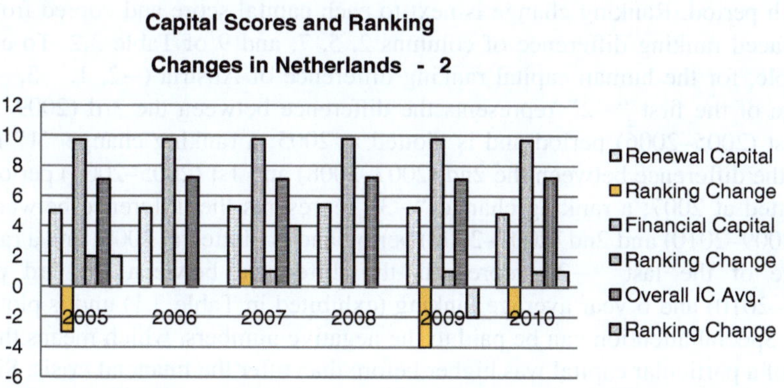

Fig. 3.22 Renewal capital, financial capital, average NIC, and ranking changes in The Netherlands

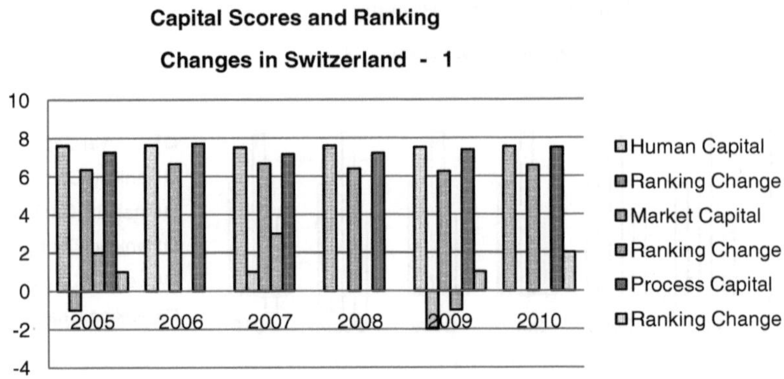

Fig. 3.23 Human capital, market capital, process capital, and ranking changes in Switzerland

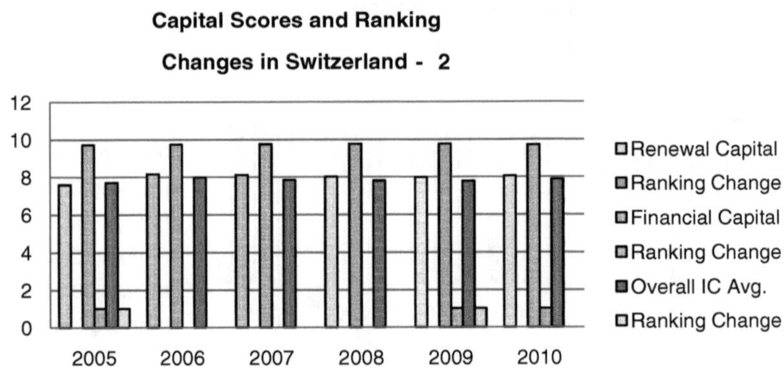

Fig. 3.24 Renewal capital, financial capital, average NIC, and ranking changes in Switzerland

The figures are mapped based on the mean capital scores and ranking changes of each period. Ranking change is next to each capital score and copied from the bold-faced ranking difference of columns 2, 5, 7, and 9 of Table 3.2. To cite an example, for the human capital ranking difference of Austria (−2, 1, −3, −2), a change of the first "−2" represents the difference between the 3rd (2009–2010) and 1st (2005–2006) period and is plotted at 2005; a ranking change "1" represents the difference between the 2nd (2007–2008) and 1st (2005–2006) period and is plotted at 2007; a ranking change "−3" represents the difference between the 3rd (2009–2010) and 2nd (2007–2008) period and is plotted at 2009; and a ranking change of the last "−2" represents the difference between the 3rd period (2009–2010) and 6 year average ranking (exhibited in Table 3.1) and is plotted at 2010. Special attention can be paid to the negative numbers, which means that the level of a particular capital was higher before than after the financial crisis. Since it is easier to read figures than tables, we will describe the finding of each figure one by one.

Table 3.2 Ranking changes in three time periods for the four small European Countries

	(1st period–3rd period)	1st period 2005–2006	2nd period 2007–2008		3rd period 2009–2010		2005–2010 average NIC48 ranking	
Human capital	Difference #1	Ranking	Ranking	Difference	Ranking	Difference	NIC 48 Ranking	Difference
Austria	**−2**	14	13	**1**	16	**−3**	14	**−2**
Belgium	**−1**	7	8	**−1**	8	**0**	8	**0**
Netherlands	**−2**	12	11	**1**	14	**−3**	12	**−2**
Switzerland	**−1**	10	9	**1**	11	**−2**	11	**0**
Market capital	Difference	Ranking	Ranking	Difference	Ranking	Difference	NIC 48 Ranking	Difference
Austria	**−10**	6	13	**−7**	16	**−3**	11	**−5**
Belgium	**−1**	23	21	**2**	24	**−3**	23	**−1**
Netherlands	**4**	7	4	**3**	3	**1**	4	**1**
Switzerland	**2**	10	7	**3**	8	**−1**	8	**0**
Process capital	Difference	Ranking	Ranking	Difference	Ranking	Difference	NIC 48 Ranking	Difference
Austria	**−4**	4	10	**−6**	8	**2**	8	**0**
Belgium	**−3**	20	19	**1**	23	**−4**	21	**−2**
Netherlands	**2**	11	8	**3**	9	**−1**	10	**1**
Switzerland	**1**	3	3	**0**	2	**1**	4	**2**
Renewal capital	Difference	Ranking	Ranking	Difference	Ranking	Difference	NIC 48 Ranking	Difference
Austria	**2**	13	12	**1**	11	**1**	12	**1**
Belgium	**0**	18	16	**2**	18	**−2**	17	**−1**
Netherlands	**−3**	12	11	**1**	15	**−4**	13	**−2**
Switzerland	**0**	1	1	**0**	1	**0**	1	**0**
Financial capital	Difference	Ranking	Ranking	Difference	Ranking	Difference	NIC 48 Ranking	Difference
Austria	**2**	10	8	**2**	8	**0**	10	**2**
Belgium	**1**	15	13	**2**	14	**−1**	14	**0**
Netherlands	**2**	8	7	**1**	6	**1**	7	**1**
Switzerland	**1**	6	6	**0**	5	**1**	6	**1**

(continued)

Table 3.2 (continued)

	(1st period–3rd period)	1st period 2005–2006	2nd period 2007–2008		3rd period 2009–2010		2005–2010 average NIC48 ranking	
NIC	Difference	Ranking	Ranking	Difference	Ranking	Difference	NIC 48 Ranking	Difference
Austria	**−2**	10	11	**−1**	12	**−1**	11	**−1**
Belgium	**−1**	18	18	**0**	19	**−1**	19	**0**
Netherlands	**2**	11	7	**4**	9	**−2**	10	**1**
Switzerland	**1**	3	3	**0**	2	**1**	2	**0**

#Remarks

1. The second column compares the 3rd (2009–2010) period ranking with the 1st (2005–2006)
2. The fifth column compares the 2nd (2007–2008) period ranking with the 1st (2005–2006)
3. The seventh column compares the 3rd (2009–2010) period ranking with the 2nd (2007–2008)
4. The last column compares the most current 3rd period ranking (2009–2010) with the original 6 year average NIC48 ranking summarized in Table 3.1

From Fig. 3.17 and Table 3.2, Austria's human capital ranking changes of −2, 1, −3, −2, shows its human capital is losing international competitiveness after the financial crisis. Its market capital ranking changes of −10, −7, −3, −5 reflects the watershed slide of its short-term NIC development presented in Figs. 3.15 and 3.16. Austria's process capital ranking changes of −4, −6, 2, 0 also indicates a relatively large-scale loss of process capital international competitiveness after the financial crisis.

Figure 3.18 and Table 3.2 show more positive results. For renewal capital and financial capital, all the ranking changes are positive. That is, Austria actually was gaining renewal capital and financial capital international competitiveness after the financial crisis. For NIC, the ranking changes were −2, −1, −1, −1 over the three time period comparisons, indicating a minor NIC competitiveness decline after the financial crisis.

From Fig. 3.19 and Table 3.2, Belgium's human capital ranking changes of −1, −1, 0, 0, shows its international competitiveness in human capital was mildly affected by the financial crisis. Its market capital ranking changes of −1, 2, −3, −1 raise a little concern. However, the last ranking change of "−1" indicates that after the financial crisis (2009–2010), its international ranking in market capital only lost one rank compared to its 6 year average, somewhat reflecting its gradual trade recovery from the financial crisis. Belgium's process capital ranking changes of −3, 1, −4, −2 deserve more attention. Belgium used to boast of its national infrastructure as a transport hub of goods and services. Yet after the financial crisis (2009–2010), its process capital competitiveness has not recovered to its 6 year average.

Figure 3.20 and Table 3.2 show relatively better ranking changes, although there are still negative numbers. Belgium's renewal capital ranking changes of 0, 2, −2, −1 and financial capital ranking changes of 1, 2, −1, 0 are relatively mild. For NIC, the ranking changes of −1, 0, −1, 0 explains that in general Belgium's NIC over the three time periods did not have too much change. Particularly, the last ranking change of "0" indicates that after the financial crisis (2009–2010), Belgium has regained its 6-year average ranking. Nevertheless, Belgium is consistently at the bottom of various types of capital among the four countries, except human capital. Lagging behind its peers in NIC is a warning sign for Belgium.

From Fig. 3.21 and Table 3.2, The Netherlands' human capital ranking changes of −2, 1, −3, −2 shows its human capital international competitiveness was modestly affected by the financial crisis. On the contrary, the all positive market capital ranking changes of 4, 3, 1, 1 reflect its strength in international trade even during and after the financial crisis. Its gaining market capital ranking throughout the financial crisis indicates that other countries were not able to withstand the impact as The Netherlands did. Its process capital ranking changes of 2, 3, −1, 1 also show its relative resilience during and after the financial crisis.

Figure 3.22 and Table 3.2 reveal The Netherlands' weakness. Its renewal capital ranking changes of −3, 1, −4, −2 show the country's weakest intangible asset. After the financial crisis, The Netherlands still did not resume its 6 year average ranking and lost its renewal capital international competitiveness. On the contrary, the financial capital ranking changes were all positive, even though its government debt and deficit increased because of the stimulus packages. For NIC, the ranking changes of 2, 4, −2, 1 were comparatively good. Particularly, the last ranking change of “1” indicates that after the financial crisis (2009–2010), The Netherlands has gained one rank over its 6 year average ranking and increased its NIC international competitiveness.

From Figure 3.23 and Table 3.2, Switzerland’s human capital ranking changes of −1, 1, −2, 0 show its human capital international competitiveness was mildly affected by the financial crisis. The last ranking change of “0” indicates that after the financial crisis (2009–2010), its human capital ranking regained its 6 year average ranking. Its market capital ranking changes of 2, 3, −1, 0 also explain the similar development as that of its human capital. The all positive process capital ranking changes of 1, 0, 1, 2 show its resilience during and after the financial crisis.

Figure 3.24 and Table 3.2 exhibit Switzerland’s all positive ranking changes. Its renewal capital ranking changes of 0, 0, 0, 0 reveal that Switzerland maintained number one ranking in renewal capital throughout the three time periods among all 48 countries. Its financial capital ranking changes of 1, 0, 1, 1 explains that Switzerland even increased its international competitiveness in financial capital during and after the financial crisis. For NIC, the ranking changes of 1, 0, 1, 0 also show Switzerland’s increasing international competitiveness in NIC.

In summary, these four small European countries did not lose much international competitiveness for their various capitals during and after the financial crisis, except Austria’s relatively large-scale market capital ranking lost. After the financial crisis, Austria gained some edge in renewal capital and financial capital; The Netherlands became even stronger in market capital and financial capital; and Switzerland excelled in process capital, renewal capital, financial capital, and NIC. Belgium had ranking gains and losses in every type of capital and did not show a particular strong area after the financial crisis.

3-Dimensional National Intellectual Capital Trajectory

Up to this point, all the figures plotted different combinations of various capitals, capital-GDP co-development, and ranking changes on a flat plane. Even though Figs. 3.7, 3.8, 3.9, 3.10, 3.11, and 3.12 displayed four dimensions with color and bubble size as the 3rd and 4th dimension in addition to X axis and Y axis, graphically they are still on one plane. This section presents three-dimensional (3D) graphs showing each country’s NIC development trajectory on a 48-country 3D landscape of various types. Since evolution over time is always complex, combining different views from different angles may provide more comprehensive perspectives.

In what follows, we first explore the value-driving context by uncovering influencing factors of GDP growth for Austria, Belgium, The Netherlands, and Switzerland from 2005 to 2010. Second, in explaining the GDP growth, we present the high, middle, and low capability which human capital, market capital, process capital, and renewal capital, respectively have. Third, we examine the efficiency (GDP growth) enhancing factors and impeding factors of each country, taking each country's turning point into consideration. Last, we identify the efficiency drivers of each country in reaching a targeted GDP.

Figure 3.25 shows a rectangular 3D landscape, with longer north–south side. The formation of the landscape is based on the data of 29 national intellectual capital indicators (presented in Appendix 3) for 48 countries covering 6 years (2005–2010), with a total of 8,352 (29 × 48 × 6) data points. In other words, Figure 3.25 is the aggregated NIC landscape of the 48 countries. The relative NIC positions of Austria, Belgium, The Netherlands, and Switzerland (pointed out with arrows) are in the upper left side of the landscape. The enlarged trails indicate the NIC progression (upward), regression (downward), or changing configuration (sideward) of each country over the 6 years. Each white trail on the landscape represents a country. The altitude coloring from purple (north), dark blue, blue,

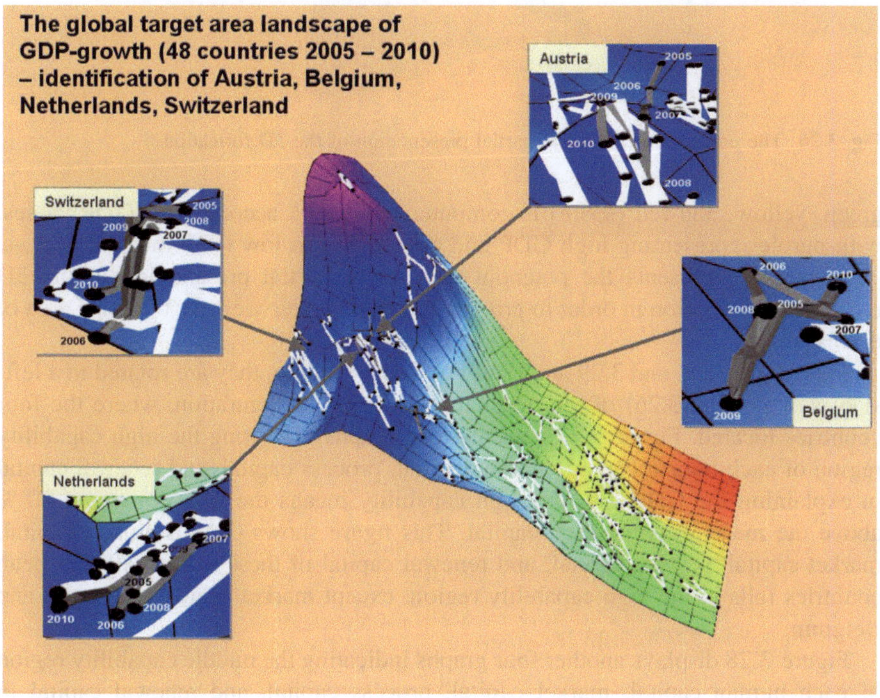

Fig. 3.25 The NIC trail of Austria, Belgium, The Netherlands, and Switzerland on a 3D 48-country landscape

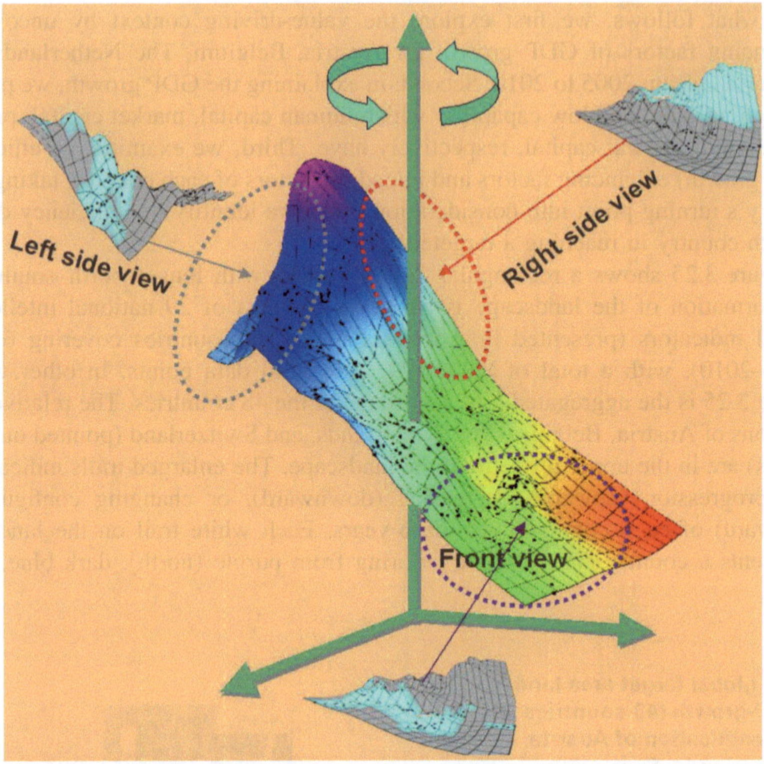

Fig. 3.26 The potential rotation and partial presentation of the 3D formation

green, yellow, and red (south) is computer generated, according to GDP values, with purple representing high GDP and descending to low GDP in red.

Figure 3.26 presents the potential rotation or partial presentation of the 3D rectangular formation in order to provide readers a better view for the focal area of discussion.

Figs. 3.27, 3.28, and 3.29 are a set. For easier reading, they are rotated to a left-side view (Figure 3.26) of the original rectangular configuration, where the four countries located. Figure 3.27 presents four graphs indicating the high capability region of each human capital, market capital, process capital, and renewal capital in explaining the GDP growth. High capability means the data points are 20 % above the mean value of each capital. This figure shows that all human capital, market capital, process capital, and renewal capital of these four small European countries falls in the high capability region, except market capital of Austria and Belgium.

Figure 3.28 displays another four graphs indicating the middle capability region of each human capital, market capital, process capital, and renewal capital in explaining the GDP growth. Middle capability means the data points are within the top 50 % value of each capital. This figure shows all human capital, market

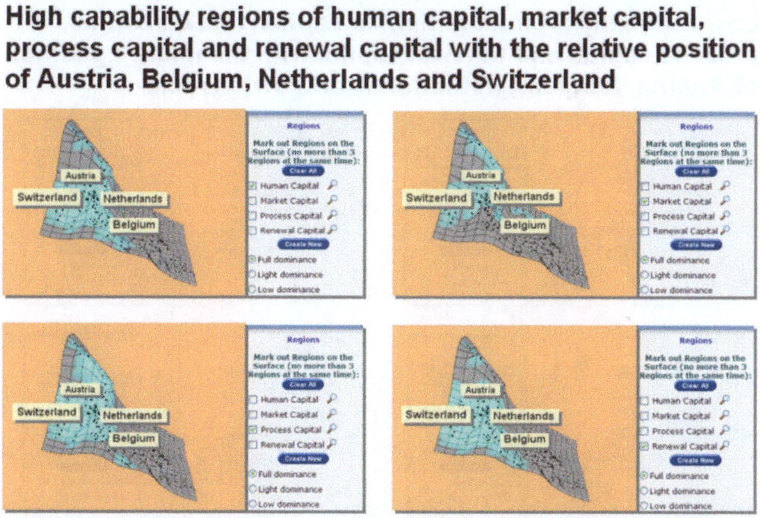

Fig. 3.27 The high capability region of human capital, market capital, process capital, and renewal capital

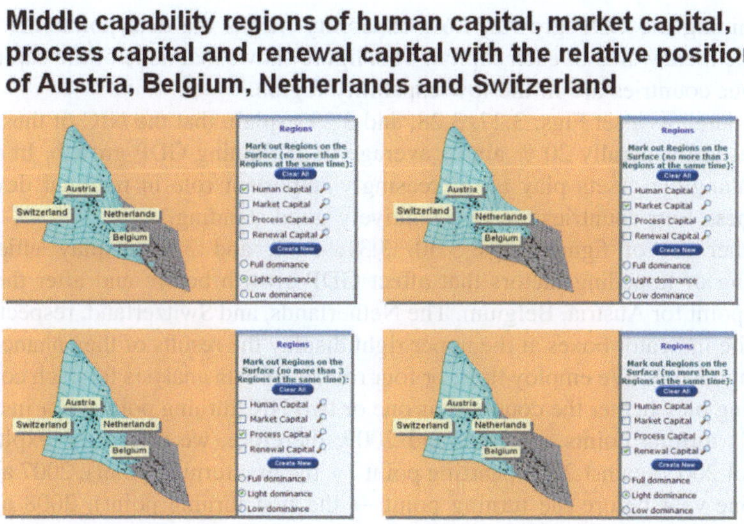

Fig. 3.28 The middle capability region of human capital, market capital, process capital, and renewal capital

capital, process capital, and renewal capital of these four countries are included in the middle capability region.

Figure 3.29 shows the last four graphs in this set indicating the low capability region of each human capital, market capital, process capital, and renewal capital

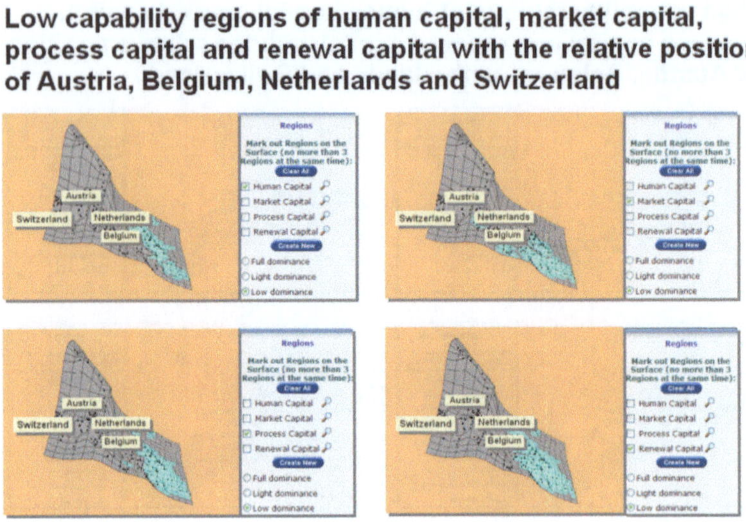

Fig. 3.29 The low capability region of human capital, market capital, process capital, and renewal capital

in explaining the GDP growth. Low capability means the data points are 20 % below the mean value of each capital. This figure shows that none of the capitals of these four countries are in the low capability region.

In general, as a set Figs. 3.27, 3.28, and 3.29 explain that the NIC of these four countries are generally 20 % above average in explaining GDP growth. In an era when intangible assets play an increasingly important role in national development, these four countries are in a relatively good standing.

Another set of figure, Figs. 3.30, 3.31, 3.32, and 3.33 display efficiency enhancing or impeding factors that affect GDP growth before and after the NIC turning point for Austria, Belgium, The Netherlands, and Switzerland, respectively. The white indicator boxes at the upper right display the results of the enhancing or impeding factors. We employ three or four rounds of data analysis for each country, depending on whether the country has one or two NIC turning points. For instance, Austria's turning points are 2008 and 2009; therefore, we traced the explaining factors of 2005 against 2008 (starting point → the first turning point), 2007 against 2008 (one year before the turning point → the first turning point), 2008 against 2009 (one year before the turning point → the second turning point), and 2009 against 2010 (the second turning point → the ending point).

For an easy reference, we summarize in Table 3.3 two sets of results, each with the first five key factors. If there is a clear score cutting point (such as less than 1 % in the white indicator boxes), the reported factors may be less than five. The first set displays the efficiency enhancing and impeding factors before the turning point, the second set exhibits the efficiency enhancing and impeding indicators after the (last) turning point in italic letters. Since the factor strength (percentage)

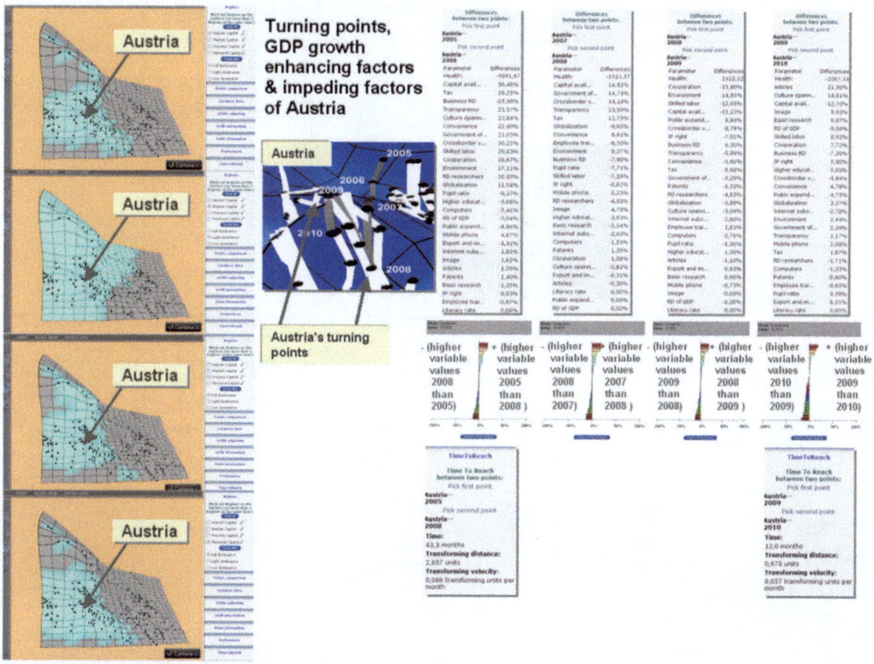

Fig. 3.30 Turning points and GDP growth enhancing and impeding factors of Austria

varies with different explaining power, we have calculated the average weight of the five enhancing and impeding factors and display each respective percentage in the rows for "Factor #5". We also count the frequency of four more frequently displayed categories, namely government-related issues (G), human capital-related issues (H), market capital-related issues (M), and research and development issues (R&D). Because capital availability was a concern during the financial crisis, we particularly highlighted this factor as "G–C."

Figure 3.30 displays the turning point (2008 and 2009), the enhancing and impeding factors of Austria. The four-rotated 3D graphs on the left hand side of the figure indicate that human capital, process capital, and renewal capital for Austria fall into the high capability region (20 % above average) and its market capital belongs to the middle capability region.

Table 3.3 shows that "capital availability" is Austria's first impeding factor before the first turning point, yet it turns into its first enhancing factor after the second turning point. This finding partially reflects the effect of its stimulus package. The frequency count of Table 3.3 shows that government-related issues (G—4 counts) hamper Austria's GDP growth the most, including capital availability, corporate tax encouragement, transparency of government policy, and convenience of establishing new firms. Market capital-related issues (M—3 counts) negatively affect its GDP growth as well, including openness of culture

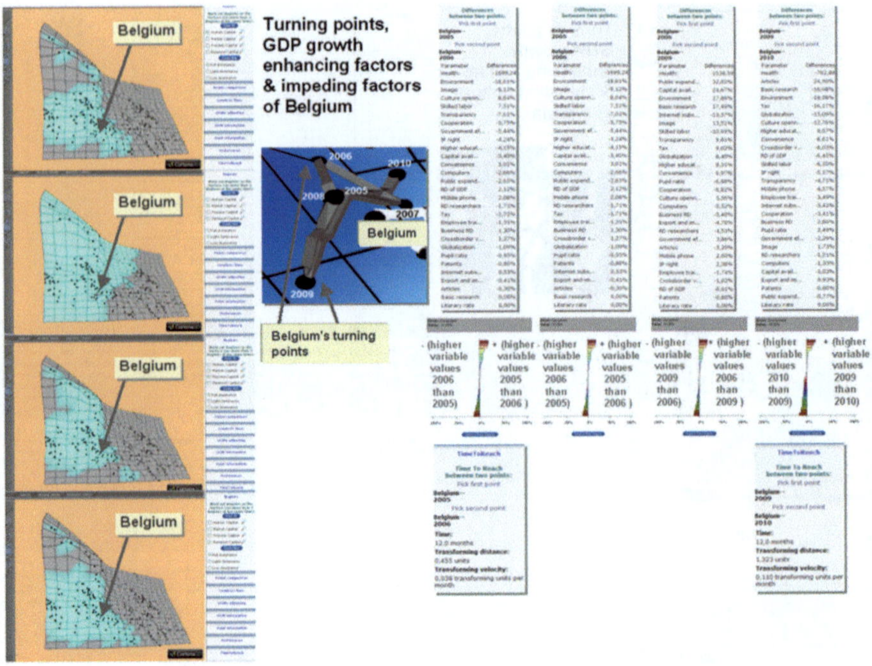

Fig. 3.31 Turning points and GDP growth enhancing and impeding factors of Belgium

and image of country. Other impeding factors, such as skilled labor, scientific articles, and basic research also deserve some attention for future improvement.

In Figure 3.31, Belgium's turning points are 2006 and 2009. The four-rotated 3D graphs on the left hand side of the figure indicate that its human capital, process capital, and renewal capital are in the high capability region (20 % above average) and market capital is in the middle capability region (top 50 %). Table 3.3 shows that "openness of culture" changed from Belgium's first impeding factor before the first turning point to the fifth enhancing factor after the second turning point. This finding indicates partial improvement of its market capital after the financial crisis. The frequency count presented in Table 3.3 shows that human capital-related issues (H—3 counts) hampers Belgium's GDP growth, including skilled labor, higher education enrollment, and employee training. Research and development issues (R&D—3 counts) negatively affect its GDP growth as well, including scientific articles, R&D % of GDP, and business R&D. Other impeding factors, such as convenience of establishing new firms also deserve some attention for future improvement.

Figure 3.32 shows three turning points for The Netherlands, 2006, 2007 and 2009. The four-rotated 3D graphs on the left hand side of the figure indicate that all the four capitals of The Netherlands are in the high capability region (20 % above average). Table 3.3 indicates that skilled labor is Netherlands' first impeding

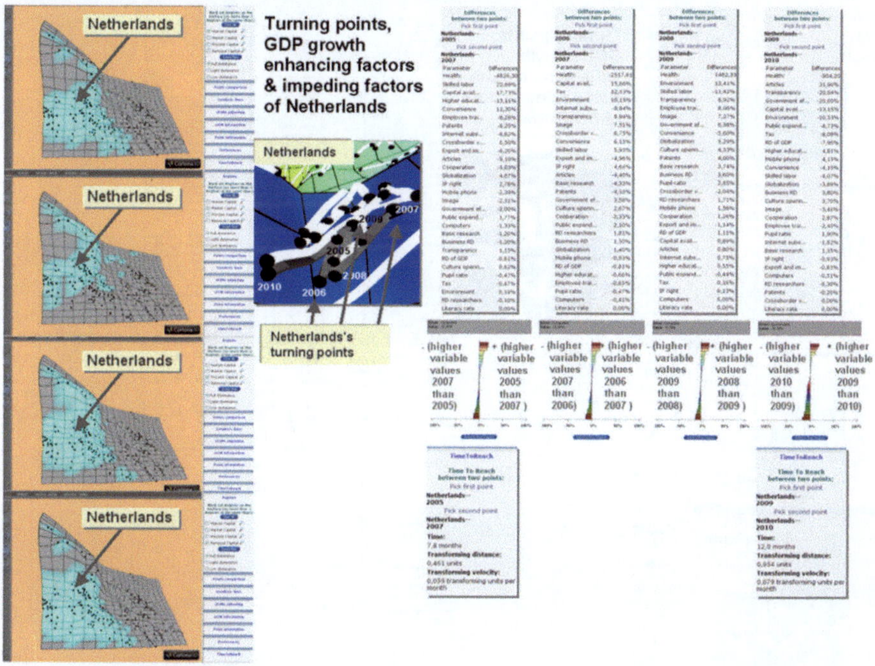

Fig. 3.32 Turning points and GDP growth enhancing and impeding factors of The Netherlands

factor before the first turning point, yet a related area employee training becomes its second enhancing factor after the second turning point. This finding may partially explain the effect of enhanced manpower training during the financial crisis, described in Chap. 2. In addition, "capital availability" is Netherlands' second impeding factor before the first turning point, yet it turns into the third enhancing factor after the second turning point. This finding partially reflects the effect of its stimulus package. The frequency count presented in Table 3.3 shows that market capital-related issues (M—3 counts) hamper Netherlands' GDP growth modestly as the fourth and fifth impeding factors, including cross-border ventures, globalization, and openness of culture. Other impeding factors, such as scientific articles and convenience of establishing new firms also deserve some attention for future improvement.

Figure 3.33 shows 2007 and 2009 are Switzerland's two turning points. The four-rotated 3D graphs on the left hand side of the figure indicate that all the four capitals of Switzerland are in the high capability region (20 % above average). The most impressive finding for Switzerland is R&D-related issues (5 counts) comprise the largest number of enhancing factors; that is, they are the main reason in explaining Switzerland's GDP growth. This result reflects its number one ranking in renewal capital among the total 48 countries. Particularly, business R&D counts twice in the 5 counts. Table 3.3 also shows that the third impeding factor—R&D

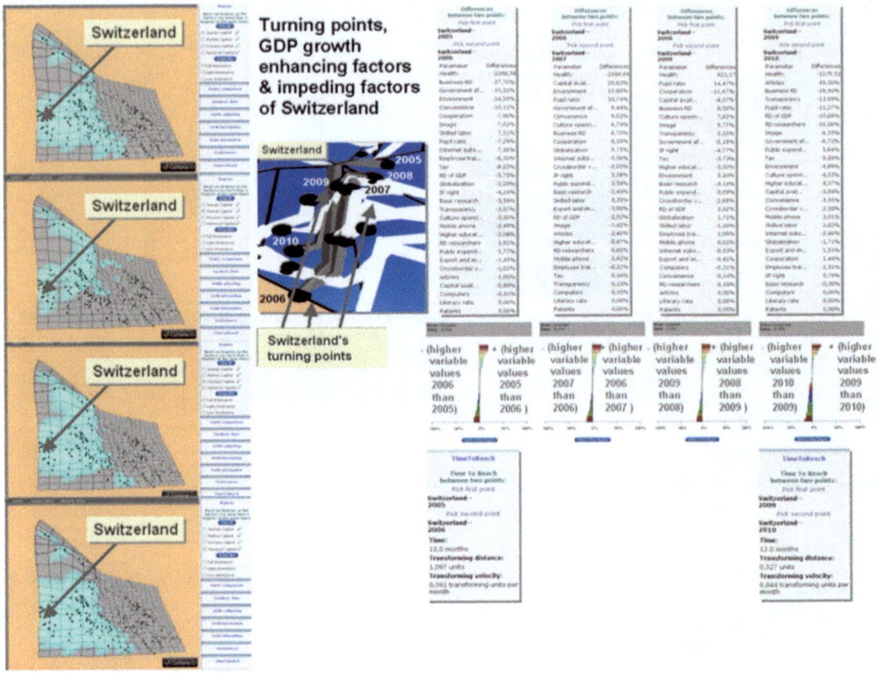

Fig. 3.33 Turning point and GDP growth enhancing and impeding factors of Switzerland

researchers before the first turning point is changed to the fifth enhancing factor after the second turning point. Yet, human capital-related issues (H—3 counts) had negative effects on its GDP growth, including skilled labor, public expenditure on education, and higher education enrollment. Other impeding factors, such as capital availability, openness of culture, and cross-border ventures also deserve some attention for future improvement.

To summarize Table 3.3 into an overall suggestion, we count the frequency of both enhancing and impeding factors by categories for all the four countries, shown in the last row of the table. There are a total of 21 counts of government-related issues (G), including 4 counts of capital availability (G-C). Among which there are 7 counts of impeding factors, including capital availability, corporate tax encouragement, transparency of government policy, and convenience of establishing new firms. Austria has a larger count (4) of government-related issues as the impeding factors.

There are 16 counts of human capital issues (H). Among which 9 counts are impeding including skilled labor, higher education enrollment, employee training, and public expenditure on education. Belgium and Switzerland have a larger count (3) of human capital issues as the impeding factors. There are 13 counts of market capital issues (M). Among these there are 8 counts of impeding factors, including openness of culture and cross-border ventures. Austria and The Netherlands have a

Table 3.3 Enhancing Factors and Impeding Factors of GDP Growth for Austria, Belgium, The Netherlands, and Switzerland

Influencing factor	Austria enhancing factors	Austria impeding factors	Belgium enhancing factors	Belgium impeding factors	Netherlands enhancing factors	Netherlands impeding factors	Switzerland enhancing factors	Switzerland impeding factors
Factor #1 before (1st) turning point	Business R&D (R&D)	Capital availability (G–C)	Fair business competition environment (G)	Openness of culture (M)	Higher education enrollment (H)	Skilled labor (H)	Business R&D (R&D)	Skilled labor (H)
Factor#1 after (last) turning point	*Capital availability* (G–C)	*Scientific articles* (R&D)	*Basic research* (R&D)	*Scientific articles* (R&D)	*Transparency of government policy* (G)	*Scientific articles* (R&D)	*Business R&D* (R&D)	*Scientific articles* (R&D)
Factor #2 before (1st) turning point	R&D researchers (R&D)	Corporate tax encouragement (G)	Image of country (M)	Skilled labor (H)	Employee training (H)	Capital availability (G–C)	Government efficiency (G)	Internet subscribers
Factor #2 after (last) turning point	*R&D % of GDP* (R&D)	*Openness of culture* (M)	*Fair business competition environment* (G)	*Higher education enrollment* (H)	*Government efficiency* (G)	*Higher education enrollment* (H)	*Transparency of government policy* (G)	*Public expenditure on education* (H)
Factor #3 before (1st) turning point	Pupil-teacher ratio (H)	Transparency of government policy (G)	Transparency of government policy (G)	Convenience of establishing new firms (G)	Patents (R&D)	Convenience of establishing new firms (G)	Fair business competition environment (G)	R&D researchers (R&D)
Factor #3 after (last) turning point	*Business R&D* (R&D)	*Image of country* (M)	*Corporate tax encouragement* (G)	*Mobile phone subscribers*	*Capital availability* (G–C)	*Mobile phone subscribers*	*Pupil-teacher ratio* (H)	*Higher education enrollment* (H)
Factor #4 before (1st) turning point	Higher education enrollment (H)	Openness of culture (M)	Enterprise-university cooperation	R&D % of GDP (R&D)	Internet subscribers	Cross-border ventures (M)	Convenience of establishing new firm (G)	–

(continued)

Table 3.3 (continued)

Influencing factor	Austria enhancing factors	Austria impeding factors	Belgium enhancing factors	Belgium impeding factors	Netherlands enhancing factors	Netherlands impeding factors	Switzerland enhancing factors	Switzerland impeding factors
Factor #4 after (last) turning point	*Cross-border venture* (M)	*Basic research* (R&D)	*Globalization* (M)	*Employee training* (H)	*Fair business competition environment* (G)	*Business R&D* (R&D)	*R&D % of GDP* (R&D)	*Cross-border ventures* (M)
Factor #5 before (1st) turning point	Computers in use per capita **(Average weight−12.41 %)** #	Convenience of establishing new firms (G) **(Average weight−26.97 %)**	Government efficiency (G) **(Average weight−9.19 %)**	Mobile phone subscribers **(Average weight−4.67 %)**	Export of goods (M) **(Average weight−8.48 %)**	Globalization (M) **(Average weight−12.78 %)**	Enterprise-university cooperation (R&D) **(Average weight−15.02 %)**	- **(Average weight−5.53 %)**
Factor #5 after (last) turning point	*Public expenditure on education* (H) **(Average weight−7.81 %)** #	*Skilled labor* (H) **(Average weight−13.01 %)**	*Openness of culture* (M) **(Average weight−16.40 %)**	*Business R&D* (R&D) **(Average weight−8.85 %)**	*Public expenditure on education* (H) **(Average weight−14.73 %)**	*Openness of culture* (M) **(Average weight−9.67 %)**	*R&D researchers* (R&D) **(Average weight−15.18 %)**	*Mobile phone subscribers* **(Average weight−12.24 %)**
Category frequency count	G-1 H-3 M-1 R&D-4	G-4 H-1 M-3 R&D-2	G-5 H-0 M-3 R&D-1	G-1 H-3 M-1 R&D-3	G-4 H-3 M-1 R&D-1	G-2 H-2 M-3 R&D-2	G-4 H-1 M-0 R&D-5	G-0 H-3 M-1 R&D-2

Remarks *(G)* & *(G–C)*—government-related issues (21 counts, including 4 counts of *G–C*), *(H)*—human capital issues (16 counts), *(M)*—market capital issues (13 counts), *(R&D)*—research and development (20 counts) larger count (3) of market capital issues as the impeding factors. For research and development issues (R&D) there are 20 counts, among which impeding factors total 9 counts, including scientific articles, basic research, R&D % of GDP, business R&D spending, and scientific articles. Belgium has a larger count (3) of R&D issues as the impeding factors.

For impeding factors, Austria (26.97 % vs. 13.01 %) and The Netherlands (12.78 % vs. 9.67 %) have higher average weights before turning points than after. Austria's large difference particularly reflects that the impeding factors were more stressful for the country before 2008. For the enhancing factors, Table 3.3 shows that most of the countries (except Austria) have higher average weights after than before their last turning point, indicating stronger enhancers after the financial crisis.

Figure 3.34 identifies the efficiency drivers (positive term) for each individual country. Efficiency targeting is akin to benchmarking. Efficiency represents GDP in this 3D software program. Since Singapore is ranked number two in financial capital among the 48 countries (surpassed by Norway only), it was identified as an ideal benchmarking target for these four countries. In Figure 3.34, the stacked small horizontal stripes are the deficiency factors of each country benchmarked against the GDP of Singapore in 2010. The length of the stripes represents the degree of deficiency. For easier comparison, we list the first five deficiency factors of each country in Table 3.4.

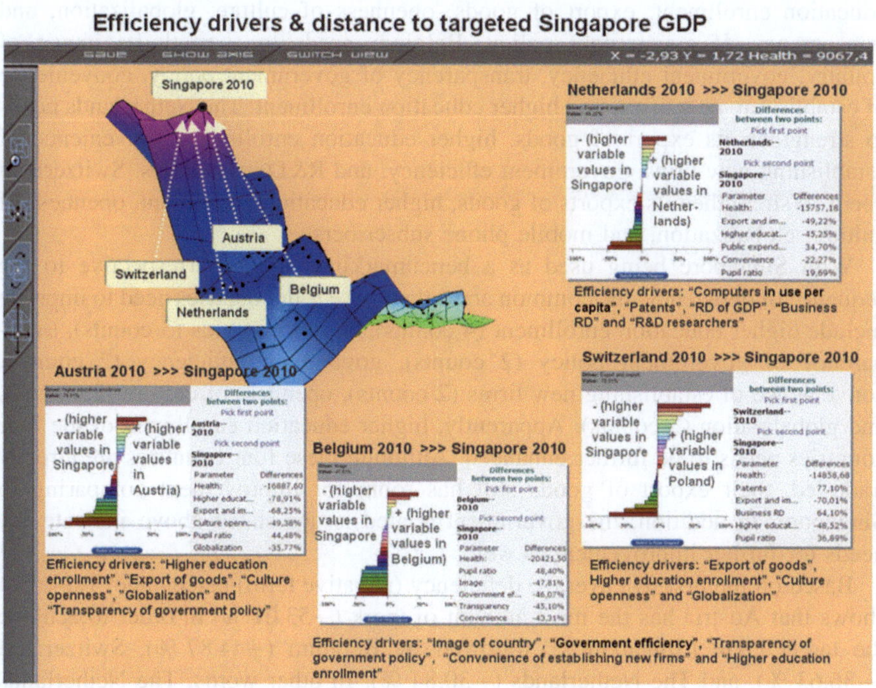

Fig. 3.34 Efficiency drivers and distance to targeted GDP of Singapore

Table 3.4 The first five efficiency drivers targeting 2010 GDP of Singapore

Efficiency driver	Austria	Belgium	Netherlands	Switzerland
Factor #1	Higher education enrollment	Image of country	Export of goods	Export of goods
Factor #2	Export of goods	Government efficiency	Higher education enrollment	Higher education enrollment
Factor #3	Openness of culture	Transparency of government policy	Convenience of establishing new firms	Openness of culture
Factor #4	Globalization	Convenience of establishing new firms	Government efficiency	Globalization
Factor #5	Transparency of government policy	Higher education enrollment	R&D researchers	Mobile phone subscribers
Average deficiency percentage of the above 5 drivers	−53.01 %	−44.87 %	−30.84 %	−36.63 %

The results indicate that Austria needs to strengthen, in sequence, its higher education enrollment, export of goods, openness of culture, globalization, and transparency of government policy. Belgium needs to strength its image of country, government efficiency, transparency of government policy, convenience of establishing new firms, and higher education enrollment. The Netherlands needs to strengthen its export of goods, higher education enrollment, convenience of establishing new firms, government efficiency, and R&D researchers. Switzerland needs to strengthen its exports of goods, higher education enrollment, openness of culture, globalization, and mobile phone subscribers.

With Singapore being used as a benchmarking country, irrespective to the sequence of deficiency, the common areas that these four countries need to improve include higher education enrollment (4 counts), export of goods (3 counts), transparency of government policy (2 counts), government efficiency (2 counts), convenience of establishing new firms (2 counts), openness of culture (2 counts), and globalization (2 counts). Apparently, higher education enrollment of the four countries needs to be further enhanced. Although these four countries are already trade-led, their export of goods still has room for improvement comparing to Singapore. In addition, the government-related issues stated above indicate the needs for further improvement as well.

Based on the first five average deficiency (negative term) percentage, Table 3.4 shows that Austria has the most amount of work (−53.01 %) in order to achieve the target GDP (Singapore's), followed by Belgium (−44.87 %), Switzerland (−36.63 %), and The Netherlands (−30.84 %). In other words, The Netherlands will have the shortest route to reach the 2010 status of Singapore. Interestingly, even though Switzerland ranks number two in NIC development among 48 countries, its route to reach Singapore's GDP level requires a longer distance than The Netherlands with NIC ranking of 10th. Raw data check reveals that Switzerland's exports and imports lagged behind that of The Netherlands a lot. As for Austria having longer distance than Belgium is mainly caused by Austria's low higher education enrollment, whereas Belgium has the best human capital in this country cluster.

The added value of the above 3D trajectory analysis is to (1) display the NIC trails of the discussed countries on a 48-country landscape; (2) locate the capability region of the four individual capitals for each country; (3) highlight NIC turning points, details of the enhancing or impeding factors, and the dynamics of factor changes for each country; and (4) calculate the distance that each country has to progress in order to achieve the benchmark GDP and identify the first five key factors to reach this goal. This section supplements the previous sections by looking into the contribution of each individual indicator in each year, rather than average scores and average rankings.

In this chapter, we reported our research findings in layman terms with graphs and tables of various types for easier reading. This study on national intangible assets has uncovered some important findings that are not apparent in other GDP-related studies. For instance, the relationship between renewal capital and GDP growth is stronger in less developed countries than in advanced countries; the distance to the same benchmarked country (Singapore) for Switzerland (−36.63 %) is actually farther than that of The Netherlands (−30.84 %), very likely due to the fact that The Netherlands is also very strong in market capital (#4), similar to Singapore.

Chapter 4
The Aftermath of 2008 Global Financial Crisis

This chapter reports activities after 2010, a time commonly regarded as the aftermath of the 2008 global financial crisis (Kehoe 2010). Although sovereign debt problems still linger in the Euro zone as of late-2012, we use 2010 as a cut-off point in order to be consistent with the reports of other country clusters in this booklet series. In what follows, we first introduce the general status of the European Union, information regarding multiple countries, and then the condition of each individual country.

Since early 2010, the Euro zone has been facing a major debt crisis. The governments of several countries in the zone accumulated what many consider to be unsustainable levels of government debt. The sovereign debt crisis developed as countries experienced higher deficits and growing debt, making governments increasingly unable to pay back the money they owed. As a result, several countries including Greece, Ireland, and Portugal had to turn to other European countries, European Central Bank (ECB), and the International Monetary Fund (IMF) for loans in order to avoid default. In June 2012, Spain also requested financial assistance.

From the statistics reported in Chaps. 2 and 3, economic situations of these four small European countries began to recover at the end of 2009 under the support of government stimulus efforts. The global financial turmoil of 2008 has not left the economies of these four countries unscathed, yet most of them have shown good recovery. Although all four countries are heavily dependent on exports, the governments' swift actions to save or nationalize the troubled banks and sufficient capital inputs have mitigated the negative impact of this financial crisis.

In September of 2011, OECD reported that major economies were tilting back into recession as sovereign debt problems continued to ail the Euro zone (Bryant 2011). With the unfolding of the debt crisis, EU member states agreed upon the establishment of a US$633.6 billion (€440 billion) Euro zone Member State-guaranteed European Financial Stability Facility (EFSF), after bailing out Greece (Moloney 2010). The EFSF will provide loans to EU member states in financial trouble. If a country receives a loan from the EFSF, it will be subject to strict austerity measures such as tax and pension reform, decreases in public wages, and

C. Y.-Y. Lin et al., *National Intellectual Capital and the Financial Crisis in Austria, Belgium, The Netherlands, and Switzerland*, SpringerBriefs in Economics,
DOI: 10.1007/978-1-4614-8021-1_4, © The Author(s) 2014

privatization of some industries. EU member states will guarantee the EFSF's bonds. Yet, the EFSF is scheduled to expire in 2013, at which time it will be replaced with a permanent crisis mechanism called the European Stabilization Mechanism (ESM). To avoid any future crises in the Euro zone, the ESM will provide loans to a member state that is threatened with severe economic difficulties and will require borrowers to follow austerity measures similar to those of the EFSF.

Concerns about the fiscal and banking problems continued to weigh on the global economic outlook. With EU countries as the major trading partners, these four small European countries faced economic slowdown again. In what follows, we briefly describe the economic status of these four countries after 2010.

Austria

Recovery has been evident for Austria since mid-May 2009, with some positive economic indicators (Ragacs and Vondra 2009). In 2010, Austria's exports of goods managed to recover from the financial crisis and rose by an astonishing 16.7 %; that is, after a decline to 50.5 % in 2009, the export revenue rose to 55.3 % GDP in 2010 (Austrian Federal Economic Chamber 2011). According to the results of simulations run with the Austrian Institute of Economic Research macroeconomic model, the relief measures taken by the federal government raised real disposable income of households by 1.6 % (Breuss et al. 2009). The recovery is also reflected by a sound labor market with an unemployment rate of 4.2 %, which is the lowest in the EU-27 (Austrian Federal Economic Chamber 2011). Austria's GDP recovered in 2010 and 2011 with growth of 2.3 and 2.9 %, respectively (U.S. Department of State 2011).

The Austrian economy has weathered the crisis well with an export-led recovery which spilled over to investment. The share of long-term unemployment and the labor force participation rate remained broadly constant through the economic downturn (Gurria 2011b). GDP has surpassed its precrisis peak in the first quarter of 2011 and its GDP per capita ranks among the highest in the Euro area (4th) and overall OECD (7th) (Gurria 2011b).

Austria's quick and smooth recovery after the 2008 global financial crisis was to a large extent made possible by economic policy measures taken by the government to stabilize the economy and to minimize the effects of the crisis (Austrian Federal Economic Chamber 2011). Private consumption was fueled by relatively high wage settlements in 2008 and by the numerous tax measures and government transfers aimed at increasing disposable household income (Ragacs and Vondra 2009). The macroeconomic effect of higher investment in infrastructure is particularly strong since the respective measures have a direct impact and are relatively labor-intensive (Breuss et al. 2009).

The stimulus measures adopted during the financial crisis has led to a short-run increase in the public debt of 73.6 % in 2011 and deficit level of 3.5 % of GDP in

2009, 4.7 % in 2010, and 3.9 % in 2011, from only about 1.3 % in 2008 (Austrian Federal Economic Chamber 2011; CIA 2012). To further strengthen the economy, Austrian government's 2012–2015 medium-term budget framework introduces legally binding spending limits to reduce the total public sector deficit to 2.0 % of the GDP in 2015 and a legal "debt brake" to reduce public sector debt to 60 % of the GDP by 2020 (U.S. Department of State 2011).

Trade with other EU-27 countries accounts for almost 72 % of Austrian imports and exports in 2010, under the Austrian economic policy of expanding trade and investment in the new EU members of central and eastern Europe (U.S. Department of State 2011). With such a trend, the Austrian Financial Market Authority (FMA) and the Austrian National Bank have decided to move up implementation of the Basel III rules, to strengthen banking groups' capital adequacy as more sustainable business models when operating in central, eastern, and southeastern Europe (U.S. Department of State 2011).

Even with Austria's promising economic outlook, OECD and International Monetary Fund (IMF) experts still called for its structural reforms in areas such as sustainability of pensions, ensuring long-term care for Austria's aging population, restructuring public sector salaries, streamlining administration, and improving the K-12 and university education systems (Fuentes 2011; U.S. Department of State 2011). Particularly, Austria needs to continue restructuring by moving to higher-quality production and emphasize knowledge-based sectors and increase research and development for future economic development (Fuentes et al. 2011). Furthermore, greater labor flexibility to encourage labor participation to offset growing unemployment, aging population, and low fertility rate are also issues of concern (U.S. Department of State 2011).

Belgium

The Belgian economy has proved more resilient than that of the Euro area as a whole, despite being strongly dependent on international trade (Meel 2009). The national accounts data reveal that the recession in Belgium was less steep than initially feared and its recovery in 2010 was faster and stronger than expected (Federal Planning Bureau 2011). In 2010, Belgian GDP grew by 2.1 %, the unemployment rate rose only slightly, and budget deficit decreased from 6 % of its GDP to 4.1 %; however, its public debt was just under 100 % of its GDP (CIA 2012). In 2011, the Belgian economy grew 0.7 % in the second quarter, outpacing growth in the Euro zone as a whole and significantly better than Germany (a meager 0.1 % growth in the second quarter) (Van de Velde 2011).

The main driver of the strong recovery in Belgium between the second half of 2009 and the first half of 2011 was the recovery led by the unexpectedly strong exports rebound in Germany (Federal Planning Bureau 2011; Van de Velde 2011). In addition, Belgium's system of automatic wage indexation—under which wages are increased in line with a rise in prices—also helped to explain the country's stronger GDP growth, which makes private consumption more resilient to a shock on inflation (Van de Velde 2011). Yet, some also suggested that the country's above-average performance was helped by the absence of austerity measures (Van de Velde 2011).

In January 2010, the Belgian government outlined its fiscal consolidation program through 2012 to preserve the sustainability of public finances while at the same time mapped out an improvement path that would not damage the fragile economic recovery (OECD 2011a; Meel 2009). Its fiscal consolidation strategy set the goal of no more than a 3 % deficit in 2012 and restoring fiscal balance by 2015 at the latest (OECD 2011a). Total fiscal saving efforts would be distributed between the federal government and regional governments based on the intergovernmental burden-sharing agreement (OECD 2011a). Although public debt was expected to fall from 2011 as most of the consolidation efforts were implemented in 2011, unfortunately Belgian public debt increased from 96.2 % in 2010 to 98.5 % in 2011 (Global Finance 2012).

To promote economic growth during fiscal consolidation, the Belgian government decided to extend some 2009 anticrisis measures to 2010, such as reducing VAT rate for construction and the implementation of new measures to stimulate employment in 2010–2011, holding part of health care resources in reserve to save 0.22 % of its GDP in 2011, decreasing 1.6 % of the state's operating costs, and saving 0.7 % on personnel expenditures. On the revenue side, the government decided to levy a tax on banks and stock exchange companies effective since January 2011 to increase revenue by 0.16 % of the GDP in 2011 (OECD 2011a). Environmental taxes, including supplemental taxes on fuel and a new taxation system for company cars based on CO_2 emissions, are estimated to supply additional revenue of US$1,251 million (€935 million) (0.26 % of GDP). Furthermore, the campaign against tax and social insurance contribution fraud will bring extra revenue of 0.1 % of its GDP (OECD 2011a).

Although Belgium is a wealthy country, public expenditure had far exceeded income for many years and taxes were not diligently pursued, which resulted in Belgium's deficit of 4.6 % in 2010 and 3.0 % in 2011 (U.S. Department of State 2012a). In addition, an aging population and rising social expenditures are mid- to long-term challenges to public finances as well (CIA 2012; IMF 2009).

In the last quarter of 2011, Belgium's economic activity marked the start of a technical recession (IHS 2012). According to the National Bank of Belgium, its leading indicator sank to a 2-year low in November 2011 and was below its long-term average in February 2012. The consumer confidence index has fallen into negative and sank to a 2.5-year low at the start of 2012. The recent sovereign credit crisis in Europe, an increased financial market volatility, an ongoing muted consumer credit conditions, and an expected tightening of fiscal policy in the coming years, are all expected to restrict growth in the near and medium terms. Near-term growth could also be negatively affected by the unstable political situation in Belgium (IHS 2012).

The Netherlands

The Dutch economy recovered slowly in 2010 with an annual growth rate of 1.8 % and 1.6 % in 2011, mainly benefitting from increased exports and growth in Germany. In 2010, exports increased by 12.8 % and imports by 11.7 %, while in 2011 the figures were 18.5 % and 19.67 %, respectively (U.S. Department of State 2012b). With the escalation of the international trade in 2010, the Dutch trade surplus grew to US$57 billion. The labor productivity increased from 3.1 % in 2009 to 3.5 % in 2010, however decreased to 2.25 % in 2011 and to an estimated 1.75 % in 2012 (U.S. Department of State 2012b). Its unemployment rate was well below the European average and had mitigated the impact of the crisis on private consumption. Labor hoarding was another contributing factor and government-subsidized temporary reduced-hours schemes had also played a role in the Dutch recovery (Enoch et al. 2011).

The financial institutions that received government aid in the midst of the crisis have almost paid back all the loans, except that the nationalized ABN Amro Bank will not be reprivatized before 2013 (U.S. Department of State 2012b). For the banking sector, the nonperformance loan ratio remained at manageable levels (<3 % of total loans) with liquid assets more than cover short-term liabilities. Profits appeared to be recovering in 2010, with a return on equity of 7 % for the sector through 2010 (Enoch et al. 2011). In 2010–2014 and beyond, the Dutch financial sector faces considerable regulatory intrusion. In particular, the Basel III proposal by the Basel Committee on Banking Supervision would boost capital requirements and liquidity ratios (EIU 2010).

The Dutch deficit was 5.4 % in 2010, but improved to 4.2 % in 2011, and a deficit of 4.5 % was projected for 2012. However, the government debt also increased rapidly from 45.5 % in 2007 to 62.8 % in 2010 and to 64.4 % in 2011 (U.S. Department of State 2012b). In order to fight against the increasing government debt and deficit levels, the government announced a spending cut by US$26 billion by 2015 (U.S. Department of State 2012b). In addition, the largest austerity measures contained the downsizing of government (US$8.5 billion), cutting back on subsidies of child daycare and rent (US$6.1 billion), significant cutbacks on defense, culture and innovation subsidies, and development cooperation (U.S. Department of State 2012b). In total, the consolidation plan amounted to around US$26.1 billion (€18 billion) or 3.3 % of its GDP, by 2015 (OECD 2011b).

Although the Dutch recovery was well under way, the economy still contracted in the second half of 2011. Domestic demand weakened as financial turmoil made investors and consumers more cautious and damaged the solvency of pension funds (OECD 2011b). In December 2011, The Netherlands Bureau for Economic Policy Analysis announced that the Dutch economy was in recession (CPB 2011). The central bank also reported that the economy contracted in the third quarter of 2011 and predicted that the Dutch economy would come to a virtual halt in 2012, with GDP growth falling to 0.2 % and unemployment rising to 5.3 % (Dutch News

2011). Such economic decline was mostly due to lower foreign trade, reduced consumers and investors spending, and the restrictive budgetary policies (CPB 2011).

The escalation of the debt crisis in the Euro zone had increasingly weighed on consumer and business sentiment. The weakening world trade growth since the second half of 2011 has prompted the Dutch government to step up its austerity program in 2012, such that the cabinet was preparing to make extra cut-off up to US$14.5 billion (€10 billion) in order to balance the government's books (Dutch News 2011). Predicted by the Dutch Rabobank, real GDP growth is expected to average 1 % during the period from 2013 to 2017, markedly lower than in the precrisis years. Consumer confidence will remain fragile and companies will be less inclined to invest, partly because it may take years before the European debt crisis is solved (Rabobank 2012).

Switzerland

Switzerland's economic activity benefited from a recovery in trade, private investment, and consumption in 2010. Its GDP grew from −1.9 % in 2009 to 2.7 % in 2010 (CIA 2012; Global Finance 2012; U.S. Department of State 2012c). Yet, its growth was reduced to 1.9 % in 2011, mainly as a result of an appreciating Swiss franc. However, due to successful government debt reduction, Switzerland was not impacted by strict austerity measures as imposed in other areas of Europe (U.S. Department of State 2012c). Overall, Switzerland managed to cut its debt from around 46.5 % in 2007 to 40.0 % in 2010, despite the peak of the crisis. In addition, even during the crisis period, the Swiss budget closed with a surplus every year (Fuentes et al. 2011). The rescue package put together by the Swiss government and the Swiss National Bank have succeeded in stabilizing its largest bank UBS, and consequently the Swiss financial sector (Fuentes et al. 2011).

Switzerland's rules-based fiscal policy contributed decisively to its low debt ratio. Its debt brake rule is a mechanism for overall management of the budget with the aim of preventing chronic deficits and rising debt levels. Discrepancies between actual expenditure and the ceiling (due to errors in the estimation of future revenues or a breach of the rule) are booked in a compensation account (Fuentes et al. 2011; OECD 2011c). For such a purpose, the Swiss constitution had already been amended in 2001 to provide for a debt brake for the federal budget (Fuentes et al. 2011). Moreover, most of the Swiss cantons have imposed budget rules of their own. The declining debt ratio brought about by these measures affords Switzerland greater room for maneuver in times of crisis and bolstered the capital markets' confidence in Swiss stability (Fuentes et al. 2011).

It is expected that the Swiss financial center will be in a better position than it was at the start of the crisis compared to other financial centers around the world. Another key factor is the important lessons learned by Switzerland from earlier crises, including the real estate crisis of the 1990s, which led to changes in governance, risk management, and compliance (Doerig 2009). As this crisis did not affect the real estate market, banks were not required to adjust their mortgage portfolios (Fuentes et al. 2011). In addition, Swiss companies' leverage is moderate in an international comparison, its robust labor market and sound government finances also fostered private and public borrowers' creditworthiness. Furthermore, low corporate taxes in Switzerland reduce companies' tax incentive for substantial debt financing (Fuentes et al. 2011).

Switzerland led the rankings of the 2011–2012 World Economic Forum's Global Competitiveness Report (Schwab 2011), reflecting the country's sound institutional environment, excellent infrastructure, efficient markets, competent macroeconomic management, world-class educational attainment, and high levels of technological innovation. All these boost Switzerland's competitiveness in the global economy (U.S. Department of State 2012c). In addition, the country has a well-developed infrastructure for scientific research. Companies spend generously on research and development (R&D) and intellectual property protection are strong (U.S. Department of State 2012c). Switzerland has successfully mitigated possible adverse effects of nonmembership by conforming many of its regulations, standards, and practices to EU directives and norms.

The Swiss financial center is today benefiting from the fact that it pursued a differentiated approach, specialized in particular fields of business (such as assets management) and underwent a consolidation at an early stage (Doerig 2009). Long-run economic growth is predicated on further structural reforms (U.S. Department of State 2012c).

Chapter 5
Future Perspective and Policy Implications

At the end of 2009, signs of recovery from the financial crisis started to show and recoveries were pretty certain in 2010 in these small European countries. Even though Euro areas are into a recession again at the second half of 2011, the positive influence of this financial crisis is it provides an ideal opportunity for a country to examine the soundness of its economic system, the effectiveness of national responses, and the profoundness of national governance.

The world will be different after this unprecedented and swift global financial impact. Radical changes are occurring in the global banking landscape, business models are being revised, the balance of power is shifting in the markets, and new rules are being negotiated—with certain parties taking a hard line (Doerig 2009). Definitely, some countries will learn from the experience and emerge to be more resilient, some will continue their structural reforms to build their future strengths, and some may still be burdened by their chronic problems. In other words, after this financial crisis, there are prospects as well as challenges.

In early 2013, more than 4 years have passed since the outbreak of 2008 global financial crisis. Although some countries in the European Union are still in deep financial troubles, it is about time to reflect what had happened during the past few years and what can be learned from this crisis for future prevention. In this chapter, we first present the prospects of these four small European countries, and then describe their potential challenges in the future. What we describe hereafter is mainly based upon the OECD economic survey report for those countries, supplemented with other relevant reports. The prospects and challenges are meant to provide points of thought or discussion and are not an exhaustive list. This chapter finishes with some policy implications.

Prospects

In January 2013, an European economic forecast stated that the worst of the crisis was over and a gradual European economic recovery will be underway before year-end (Lachman 2013). Back in mid-2012, European Central Bank (ECB) has

C. Y.-Y. Lin et al., *National Intellectual Capital and the Financial Crisis in Austria, Belgium, The Netherlands, and Switzerland*, SpringerBriefs in Economics,
DOI: 10.1007/978-1-4614-8021-1_5,

announced the commitment of the ECB to do whatever it took to save the Euro and to substantially bring down European government borrowing costs. In supporting this promising view, the prospect of each country is described hereunder.

Austria

Austria enjoys an outstanding quality of life. In the comparison of the EU-27 and an additional four countries (Croatia, Macedonia, Turkey, and Norway), Austria holds the first place for the quality of health services, the third place in the availability and quality of public transport, the fifth place in employment, and the sixth place with respect to low-wage differentials (Austrian Federal Economic Chamber 2011). After the financial crisis, Austria became more resilient and prosperous mainly due to its workforce, integration with EU, government policies, research and development (R&D), green environment, and trade relationship. These features are described hereunder:

Workforce: Austria has a highly skilled and motivated labor force, which manifests itself in low unemployment and, in particular, low youth unemployment (Gurria 2011b). In addition, Austrian business social partners, such as labor union, go beyond their traditional role of negotiating wages and work conditions by taking responsibility for preparing reform proposals (Gurria 2011b).

Integration with EU: The introduction of the Euro was an additional boost with additional positive effects on Austrian economic and trade growth, also on price stability and the labor market. For the trade flows, around 83 % of Austrian exports go to Europe (70 % to EU partners) with Germany being its main trading partner of around 30 % exports and 40 % imports (Austrian Federal Economic Chamber 2011). As a small and open economy, Austria takes great advantage of the huge EU internal market with a population of over 500 million people. Being in the center of Europe, Austria secures its international competitiveness and strengthens its attractiveness as a business location (Austrian Federal Economic Chamber 2011). In Austria, both companies and citizens benefit from free trade within EU and the elimination of customs controls. Furthermore, they can operate on a huge economic market with a large variety of consumption opportunities (Austrian Federal Economic Chamber 2011).

Government policies: Austria's international orientation and tradition of strong property rights are the backbone of its economic growth. The government has streamlined time-consuming regulations, and a comprehensive legal framework that promotes competition. Foreign investment requirements are not particularly stringent, and the financial market facilitates entrepreneurial activity. In general, the corporate tax regime is competitive (Heritage 2011). In addition, Austria has endorsed the OECD standard for the exchange of information in tax matters. Thus, Austria is in a position to exchange information on all tax matters foreseeably relevant for the administration or enforcement of the domestic law of its treaty partners (OECD 2009a). Other than that, Austrian pension reforms adopted between 2001 and 2005 kept the rise in pension expenditures relatively low, making it the fourth-lowest real increase in average pensions in the period from 2007 to 2060 within the EU (Reiss and Kohler-Toglhofer n.d.) Furthermore, during the financial crisis about 29 % of all Austrian stimulus measures of 2009 and 2010 is classified as forward-looking and about 22 % was for infrastructure investment (with heavy emphasis on green technologies and energy-saving insulation of buildings) (Breuss et al. 2009). All the above measures facilitate building a better government finance. After the financial crisis, there is also widespread political consensus that education, science, and research must be considered high priorities and be funded appropriately. Accordingly, 1 % of the GDP is to be allocated to basic research and 2 % to the tertiary education sector with investments climbing to at least US$3.2 billion (€2.5 billion) by 2020 (Kratky 2012).

R&D: Austria's gross domestic expenditure for R&D is among the highest in the EU, amounting to US$9.8 (€7.89 billion) or 2.78 % of the GDP in 2010. It is steadily moving towards the goal of spending at least 3 % of its GDP (Austrian Federal Economic Chamber 2011). In 2011, the private sector accounts for more R&D expenditures than the federal state. Austrian companies are more progressive than the European average: 44 % of small and 71 % of medium sized enterprises directly engage in innovation activities (Austrian Federal Economic Chamber 2011). They are also among Europe's best in implementing the results of R&D into their day-to-day work.

Green environment: In Austria, over 30 % of energy consumption is covered by renewable energy sources and over 65 % of electricity is produced by renewables, both well over the EU average. Hydro power has the largest share, followed by wind energy. In addition, Austria has pledged itself to the European climate and energy package (the so-called "20-20-20 goals"). This corresponds to national climate and several energy goals to be achieved by 2020, such as increase the share of renewable energy to 34 %, reduce CO_2 emissions by a minimum of 16 %, and increase energy efficiency by 20 % (Austrian Federal Economic Chamber 2011).

Trade relationship: Austria has close trade relationship with the EU as well as a wide range of countries in different regions. According to Austrian Federal Economic Chamber (2011), Italy, Switzerland, the U.S., France, and the Czech Republic are also its important trade partners, in addition to Germany. The central and east European (CEE) region, the BRIC countries, South Africa, and Turkey become more and more important export markets for Austrian companies. The high export growth rates countries include Brazil (+34 %), Russia (+22 %), China (+40 %), and Turkey (+40 %). 2011 report shows that exports to the CEE region have risen to around US$21.8(€15 billion), which corresponds to a fourfold increase compared to 1995 (Austrian Federal Economic Chamber 2011).

Belgium

With exports and imports approximately equal to its GDP, Belgium depends heavily upon world trade (U.S. Department of State 2012a). Belgium's trade advantages are derived from its central geographic location and a highly skilled, multilingual, and productive workforce. To exploit these advantages, Belgium developed an excellent transportation infrastructure of ports, canals, railways, and highways to integrate its industry with that of its neighbors. Although without natural resources, Belgium imports raw materials and semi-finished goods that are further processed and re-exported. As a result, most traditional industrial sectors are represented in the economy, including steel, textiles, refining, chemicals, food processing, pharmaceuticals, automobiles, electronics, and machinery fabrication. Despite the heavy industrial component, services account for 77.4 % of GDP in 2009 (U.S. Department of State 2012a). These developments have built solid economic foundation for Belgium.

In the increasingly global economy, Belgium's high internationalization poses an advantage. U.S. and other foreign companies in Belgium account for approximately 11 % of the total workforce, with the U.S. share at about 6 % (U.S. Department of State 2012a). U.S. companies are heavily represented in the chemical sector, automotive assembly, petroleum refining, and pharmaceutical sectors. A number of U.S. service industries followed in the wake of these investments such as banks, law firms, public relations, accounting, and executive search firms. Attracted by the EU 1992 single-market program, many U.S. law firms and lawyers have settled in Brussels since 1989 (U.S. Department of State 2012a). These features help Belgium build a multi-culture and pro-trading environment.

For future development, the Belgium government greatly promotes energy saving under its green certificate policy. In 2010, Belgium has become one of the 10 largest PV (photovoltaic) markets in the world (Seefeld 2012) with Brussels hosted the Solar Future Belgium II in March 2012.

The Netherlands

In 2011, Dutch financial soundness has improved compared to that of 2008. The medium-term expenditure framework has been planned and strict adherence has facilitated and secured implementation of the consolidation plan over the time period for a better recovery (OECD 2011b). De Nederlandsche Bank (DNB) was making intensive and well-focused efforts to redress earlier shortcomings with the result that all large banks maintain capitalization buffers well above minimum requirements after the financial crisis. The capital augmentation and general return to profitability has positioned the banks well to meet higher Basel III requirements (Enoch et al. 2011).

To further reform the financial system, the government has adopted an objective-based "twin peaks" supervisory model for coping with the increasingly blurred conventional credit/insurance/securities boundaries. Under this model, DNB became a single prudential supervisor for all financial institutions (banks, insurance companies, investment firms, pension funds, and securities firms) as one peak. The second peak is the Authority for Financial Markets (AFM), which was created as a supervisor responsible for conduct-of-business supervision with a strong focus on market behavior and consumer/investor protection (Enoch et al. 2011). This model was based on the view that the objective of prudential supervision is to safeguard financial stability, while the objective of conduct-of-business supervision is to protect consumers. With micro and macroprudential oversight concentrated in one institution, DNB has the ability to take a systemic view, which allowed it to react quickly and decisively to address the crisis. This structure also grants DNB power to appoint, instruct, and dismiss official administrators on the basis of qualitative and quantitative triggers (Enoch et al. 2011).

After the financial crisis, exit from state support is proceeding as planned and remains broadly appropriate, as several financial institutions have partially repaid the state for equity injections following successful capital issuances (Enoch et al. 2011). To reduce deficit and government debt, the Dutch government started its consolidation by withdrawing the stimulus, reducing public administration costs, raising the retirement age in the state pension system, cutting health care, and implementing higher property taxes (OECD 2010). The plan stipulates a minimum of 0.5 % of GDP structural improvement per year, until a structural balance is reached (OECD 2010). If a fiscal surplus is expected to take place every year over the medium term, 50 % of the surplus will be used for paying off public debt and 50 % will be used for tax reliefs (OECD 2011b).

The Dutch economy also has well-grounded service industries that can be further developed. For example, its asset management sector is large, modern, and well managed. Besides pension funds, a considerable range of investment funds is available, including equity funds, bond funds, real estate funds, hedge funds, mixed funds, and others. At end of 2009, investment funds (excluding pension funds and insurers) had assets under management of US$475 billion with the largest fund allocations in shares and other securities (EIU 2010). In addition, the government strives to improve the investment environment in The Netherlands with the corporate tax rate of 25.5 %, which is well below the EU average. Dividend tax has been reduced from 25 % to 15 %. The Netherlands also offers participation exemption and a 30 % tax break for highly qualified foreign employees (QFinance n.d.a)

For natural resources, in 2009 The Netherlands was the second-largest producer and the second-largest net exporter of natural gas in Europe (both after Norway). The port city of Rotterdam is one of the world's major centers for crude oil imports, trading, refining, and petrochemical production and Europe's largest port in terms of cargo tonnage (Heritage 2012; U.S. Department of State 2012b). The Netherlands' goal is to become a gas "roundabout" for the Western Europe, a hub that gathers natural gas from various sources (including the North Sea, Algerian, and Qatari liquefied natural gas), and then distributes it via pipeline to continental Europe (U.S. Department of State 2012b).

Furthermore, the Dutch government works closely with industry and nongovernmental organizations to reach environmental targets. It welcomed the EU's 2008 directive to cut greenhouse gas (GHG) emissions 20 % from 1990 levels and increase power derived from renewable sources to 20 % by 2020. The Netherlands has a binding national target to reduce emissions in sectors not covered by the EU emissions trading system by 16 % in 2020. It also has a binding national target of 14 % in 2020 for renewable energy (U.S. Department of State 2012b). The above-stated features may facilitate bright future prospects in The Netherlands.

Switzerland

During the financial crisis, Switzerland succeeded in stabilizing the banking sector without unduly burdening government budgets (Fuentes et al. 2011). The financial sector is a central pillar of the Swiss economy. It plays a key transmission role within the economy as a whole, optimizing the allocation of capital as a factor of production. In efficiently allocating capital and risk and ensuring a sufficient supply of credit, the financial sector provides an important prerequisite for the economy to exploit its growth potential (Swiss Federal Council 2009). After the crisis, Switzerland can build upon its advantages of legal system, financial system, business environment, and manpower for future development. These features are described hereunder:

Legal system: The Swiss legal system is highly developed, commercial law is well-defined, and solid laws and policies protect investments well (U.S. Department of State 2012c). In addition, it has a long tradition of legal certainty and protection of property rights which creates a secure environment for business.

Financial system: Switzerland is known for its high standard of banking and financial services and has earned a solid reputation as a safe haven. With decades of a relatively strong Swiss franc, traditionally unrestricted convertibility, the absence of currency reforms, the Swiss franc is one of the world's soundest currencies (U.S. Department of State 2012c). In addition, its well-known banking secrecy meant that persons and institutions domiciled abroad could benefit unreservedly from the advantages of the Swiss financial center with respect to their assets in Switzerland under the protection of the Swiss legal system (Swiss Federal Council 2009). For the post-crisis period, it appears that Switzerland has even better opportunities to further strengthen its role as a leading global financial center, since the enduring qualities that contributed to its success are now more sought after than ever (Doerig 2009). As a financial center, Switzerland is in a relatively strong position to prepare for the future and to enhance its competitiveness (Doerig 2009).

Business environment: Switzerland as a financial center offers certain traditional strengths, such as the country's political stability, the rule of law, an efficient judicial system independent of political influence, the absence of corruption, high levels of transparency and accountability within public institutions, the dependability of public sector bodies, functioning institutions, a reliable infrastructure, low interest rates, and inflationary pressures are under control (Heritage 2012; Swiss Federal Council 2009; U.S. Department of State 2012c). All of these sustain vibrant entrepreneurship and business activity for business to benefit from such well-developed institutional framework. Switzerland also provides competitive tax burden for legal entities and natural persons alike (Swiss Federal Council 2009). Such protection of foreign bank clients has helped make Switzerland the world's largest manager of cross-border assets (Swiss Federal Council 2009). The Swiss financial center has all the structural prerequisites to maintain its global leadership position in several financial areas. An added advantage is that Swiss banks can utilize the foreign capital to benefit Swiss SMEs in the form of financing (Doerig 2009). Swiss government also has an agreement with EU known as the "Bilateral" to help its businesses, as the EU is Switzerland's largest trading partner with 59 % of its exports and 75 % of its imports in 2010 (U.S. Department of State 2012c).

Manpower: With decades of international financial services, Switzerland's workforce has become more international and open. That is, Switzerland has flexible labor regulations and a broad sector of the population that is highly educated. Higher education and training are rapidly growing in importance as engines of productivity growth in Switzerland (Heritage 2012; U.S. Department of State 2012c). Almost all workers are educated at least to the upper secondary level and vocational education contributes to one of the most successful transition performances of youth to employment in the OECD (2009b). Higher education enjoys an excellent reputation, as reflected in one of the highest scientific publication rates relative to population in the OECD and high placements of Swiss universities in international rankings. Swiss participation in continuous education is among the largest in the OECD (2009b).

Challenges

Although the 2008 global financial crisis was declared over, the Euro zone debt crisis and European recession which started in the second half of 2011 are standing in the way of the economic recovery in Europe. Economists also foresee a number of weak years on the horizon even once the Euro zone crisis has been solved, in part due to the possibilities that economic stimulus have been exhausted (Rabobank 2012). In an early 2013 prediction, the European crisis is likely to intensify since the prospective fiscal policy tightening will be occurring when the European banks continue to restrict credit and the global economic environment is souring (Lachman 2013). Adding each country's internal factors, challenges are still ahead as described hereunder.

Austria

In the post-crisis period, Austria can continue its reforms to become an even more resilient country, if they attend to the issues of lower debt and deficit levels, reforms, aging population, health care system, and education elaborated hereunder.

Lower debt and deficit levels: Economic recovery alone will not suffice to lower Austria's debt and deficit levels; therefore, considerable consolidation measures are needed to bring the debt to GDP ratio below 60 %, to take more frontloaded action in meeting foreseeable medium to long-term spending pressures, and to seek efficiency gains in all major spending areas (Gurria 2011b).

Reforms: The Austrian Federal Economic Chamber (2011) reported that reforming the pension and social system, the health sector and structural, as well as administrative reforms have become priorities for the federal government. The post-crisis period offers a golden opportunity to strengthen reform efforts, including subsidized avenues into early retirement should be eliminated, work incentives of low skilled workers should be strengthened and their cost of employment reduced, early child care infrastructure and full day schooling should be expanded to raise female labor supply, and competition should be further enhanced in network services as well as in liberal professions (Gurria 2011b; Reiss and Kohler-Toglhofer n.d.). Tax reform is also a pressing issue, as taxation of property in Austria is much lower than elsewhere in the OECD. The tax burden should be turned away from labor and entrepreneurship toward less distortive taxes such as those on property (Gurria 2011b). Austria should also make full use of the performance budgeting framework that it plans to introduce from 2013, for more assertive spending prioritization and cost-benefit checks (Gurria 2011b). For instance, Austria's above EU average spending on R&D needs to be monitored for the final outcome. To increase potential output by raising aggregate productivity, possible measures include improving the supply of risk capital, a reform of the financing of universities, fostering competition in the service sector, increasing price transparency, and offering more resources for regulators (Reiss and Kohler-Toglhofer n.d.).

Aging population: Austria's aging society constitutes a further risk to the long-term sustainability of public finances. By estimation, the additional costs arising from aging would be higher than the additional costs created by the global economic crisis (Reiss and Kohler-Toglhofer, n.d.). The average retirement age in Austria is among the lowest in the OECD, therefore the policy of later retirement should be considered (Gurria 2011b). In addition, greater labor flexibility and active labor participation to offset Austria's aging population and low fertility rate should also be encouraged (CIA 2012).

Health care system: The highly regarded Austrian health system is very expensive and will face growing pressures in the future (Gurria 2011b). In addition, the current governance and funding structure of the system is excessively fragmented, which makes too much use of inpatient care in hospitals and individual agents have incentives that conflict with overall system efficiency (Gurria

2011b). Without important structural reforms, it may be difficult to maintain the quality and social equity in the system, as the population ages and health technologies become more costly (Gurria 2011b). Coping measures include clear performance criteria, clear responsibilities of financing and spending across government layers, national capacity plan for inpatient and outpatient care enforcement, performance-based payment mechanisms, free competition in the pharmaceutical market, disease management in all chronic care areas, and spending projections and scenarios of the medium-term fiscal outlook (Gurria 2011a). In addition, more emphasis is needed on healthy lifestyles, as lifestyle factors are generally not supportive of good health outcomes that put additional pressure on costs (Gurria 2011b).

Education: OECD (Gurria 2011b) commented that for Austria to ensure its place in the Champions League, further focus on productivity, labor markets, and education is needed. Despite impressive progress in catching up to other countries, Austria still lags behind significantly in terms of scientific output compared to nations of similar size and wealth, such as Switzerland, The Netherlands, Sweden, Finland, and Denmark (Kratky 2012). In addition, a below-average number of academic degrees were conferred in Austria (approximately 2,800 per million inhabitants, compared to more than 4,000 in Switzerland and 6,500 in The Netherlands). There is also a low percentage of university graduates—Austria's percentage (18 %) is well below the OECD average of 27 % and the country is also at the bottom of the table in terms of the share of highly qualified immigrants (11.3 %) (Kratky 2012). Therefore, education reforms should continue (Gurria 2011b).

Belgium

Although Belgium recovered even better than Germany after the financial crisis (Van de Velde 2011), its long-term challenge is the separation of the north Flanders and the south Wallonia. The existing fiscal federalism arrangements are creating unsustainable imbalances. Its structural rigidities persist, dampening growth, impeding job creation, and eroding Belgium's competitive position in the world (IMF 2009). Therefore, consideration should be given to reforming the current fiscal federalism framework to improve its efficiency and effectiveness, with a view to providing a better match between spending authority and revenue raising responsibilities. The IMF (2009) also suggests that the current arrangements involving informal agreements between federal and community/regional governments should be converted into internal stability pacts that would be debated by legislatures as part of the regular budget cycle, be published, and have sanctions for noncompliance.

Belgium's lingering structural weaknesses hinder reforms for enhancing economic freedom and international competitiveness. Its tax system is burdensome and the extensive welfare led to high government spending with government's debt burden soaring around 100 % of its GDP (Gurria 2011c; Heritage 2012). With the baby boom generation approaching retirement, pension, and other social entitlement programs have become a major concern. As a result, a renewed and sustained effort to prefund aging costs is needed, including revisiting intergovernmental prefunding agreements (U.S. Department of State 2012a). Thus, well-designed plans for spending restraint and better control of aging-related cost increases are also needed. In addition, youth minimum wage should be increased more gradually and better integration of immigrants requires better language training and adapting education to their needs (Gurria 2011c).

Despite some progress, labor market rigidities remain a considerable barrier to productivity and job growth in Belgium (Heritage 2012). IMF (2009) encourages Belgium authorities to press ahead with labor market reforms so as to boost participation rates and reduce unemployment. Belgian national unemployment figures mask considerable differences between Flanders and Wallonia. Unemployment in Wallonia is mainly structural, while in Flanders it is cyclical. Flanders' unemployment level equals only half that of Wallonia. The southern region continues a difficult transition out of sunset industries (mainly coal and steel), while sunrise industries (chemicals, high-tech, and services) that dominate in Flanders have labor shortages (Tanuro 2008; U.S. Department of State 2012a).

Since future economy is energy and emission intensive, making energy policies the keys to greener growth is essential. Environmental taxation, particularly low in Belgium, should be the main tool to deal with these issues (Gurria 2011c). Negative transport externalities should be addressed by fuel taxation, road pricing, and congestion charges, as well as a scaling down of measures promoting commuting and company cars. Measures to improve thermal efficiency of housing should be refocused on low-income households. There is also a need for reviewing the division of environmental responsibilities to reduce the costs of lack of coordination and harmonization of policies. Water policies would also be more efficient with better internalizing pollution costs in water charges (Gurria 2011c).

Furthermore, Belgian exporters have been losing market share since 1995, as they export mainly to slower growing economies, without enough specialization in high-value added products, leading to eroding competitiveness in unit labor costs (IMF 2009). So far, Belgian fiscal policy has responded to the short-term challenges, but a medium-term consolidation strategy that can address aging-related and sustainability issues has not yet been announced (IMF 2009). In addition, further Euro weakness and the potential for a fresh rally in global energy prices could keep Belgian inflation elevated (Market Research 2012).

The Netherlands

For the Dutch government, even though the financial soundness has improved vulnerabilities remain. Its short-term challenge is to exit from stimulus policies and fiscal consolidation should be combined with structural reforms to boost employment and participation rates. Its most crucial longer term challenges are to secure fiscal sustainability and raise potential growth in an aging society (OECD 2010). Specifically, the challenges are largely pertaining to aging issues, reducing debt and deficit, financial sector reform, governance issues, and labor force issues elaborated hereunder.

Aging issues: A particular challenge for the Dutch government is to restrict growth in aging-related spending, such as health and pensions (OECD 2010). According to OECD (2010), the total costs of aging for the Dutch budget, relative to the GDP, are set to increase by over 9 % points between 2010 and 2060, the fifth highest in the EU and double the EU average. The costs of long-term care, already the highest in the EU, are expected to rise by 4.6 % points—four times the EU average. The expected 4 % point increase in pension spending is also above the EU average. These estimates are likely to increase in response to the upward revision in life expectancy. With respect to pensions, the government should increase the official retirement age by 2–67 years, and more front-loading of this measure would have stronger effects on fiscal sustainability and reduce early retirement incentives in the transition phase (OECD 2010). The main concern is the generosity of the Dutch system. The increases in aging-related spending need to be curbed to secure fiscal sustainability (OECD 2010).

Reducing debt and deficit: Government spending remains high and public finance sustainability has deteriorated following the crisis. Consolidation should primarily aim at curbing growth in public spending (OECD 2010). In a Database for Institutional Comparisons in Europe Report, two Dutch professors suggest various ways in which the sustainability gap can be reduced without raising taxes as briefly explained hereunder (Beetsma and Gradus 2010). Improvements in the economic structure, such as more R&D and a better educated labor force can raise labor productivity. About one-sixth of the sustainability gap can be eliminated by reducing public sector wages. And an important fraction of the gap can be filled by a more efficient public administration, estimating a deficit reduction of 1.25 % of the GDP amounting to 25 % savings on the expenses of public administration. Important reforms should include the streamlining of administrative processes and administrative bodies, fewer rules and inspections, simplified tax system, and restricted subsidies. Furthermore, government deficit can be reduced by reforming the health care sector, by separating the provision of accommodation from that of long-term care, by transferring curative care to the Health Insurance Law, and by transferring the responsibility for support to the local authorities. They propose that a structural deficit reduction can be achieved through the above measures (Beetsma and Gradus 2010).

Financial sector reform: Although the Dutch financial institutions have improved their soundness after the financial crisis, their short-term challenges to the system include internal high indebtedness of home buyers and external factors. Dutch households remain heavily indebted, amongst the highest in the EU, with the most lending relates to housing encouraged by generous mortgage interest deductibility (Enoch et al. 2011). As the average loan-to-value ratio is high, well above 100 %, macroprudential instruments should be developed to lower the system's vulnerability. The key external risk stems from the sizable cross-border activities of Dutch financial institutions and the local activities of foreign-owned financial institutions, which require closer scrutiny and supervisory engagement (Enoch et al. 2011). Therefore, legislative reforms will be needed to strengthen crisis management and bank resolution capacity, including changes to the deposit guarantee scheme.

Governance issues: To strengthen future governance, the following measures should be considered (Enoch et al. 2011; OECD 2010). First, establish routine reporting requirements to strengthen monitoring and risk modeling; second, intensify supervision of large international financial institutions with greater emphasis on group supervision and soundness of business models are required; third, develop a communication plan on recent and prospective changes in payouts to stakeholders; fourth, strengthen the institutional framework for crisis management by shifting decision-making power from the Judiciary to DNB in the context of bank resolution and by specifying more clearly the respective roles of the Ministry of Finance and DNB in bank resolution; and fifth, improve macroprudential regulation and supervision of financial markets in cooperation with international institutions. In addition, regulatory reporting suffers from a lack of timeliness, and quarterly returns are not formalized. Therefore, consistent and sufficiently comprehensive information should be strengthened to better inform offsite monitoring and to increase capacity for early warning (Enoch et al. 2011).

Labor force issues: Labor utilization remains relatively low in The Netherlands, reflecting relatively high participation combined with low hours worked, despite a strengthening of activation policies over the past couple of years (OECD 2010). Measures could aim at lengthening working careers by offering wage subsidies for hiring older workers and older workers should be encouraged to continue to work through tax incentives. Younger people (<27 years) are no longer eligible for passive income support, but are encouraged to work or study. Moreover, there is a need to increase the hours worked by females.

Switzerland

Although Switzerland has weathered this financial crisis better than other countries, the Swiss financial center is vulnerable through its high dependency on cross-border asset and wealth management with its comparatively small domestic market (Swiss Federal Council 2009). While the Swiss financial regulatory apparatus has been greatly improved during this decade, further steps need to be taken to better contain the systemic risks (OECD 2009b). Challenges are largely related to financial regulation, losing foreign markets, international cooperation, political system, and bilateral agreement described hereunder.

Financial regulation: In Switzerland, the dominance of the two big banks and the major insurance companies pose a cluster risk for the economy, combined with a moral hazard problem, given the implicit state guarantee (Swiss Federal Council

2009). The comparatively large magnitude of the losses of its two largest banks in relation to capital has underscored the systemic risks to the economy posed by the institutions' large size relative to Swiss GDP and their extensive cross-border and cross-currency activities (OECD 2009b). Therefore, it is important for Switzerland to draw up a set of "macro prudential" regulatory instruments suited to rapidly identifying and defusing stability risks arising from undesirable systemic developments (Fuentes et al. 2011). Particularly, prudential standards for the two largest Swiss banks will need to be above the average maintained by their peers in other countries. Macroprudential oversight needs to be further strengthened and broadened (OECD 2009b).

Losing foreign markets: The greatest threat facing the Swiss financial center is the risk of Swiss financial institutions losing access to foreign markets (Swiss Federal Council 2009). There are certain trends acting as a barrier to cross-border market access for Swiss financial institutions or products, such as tax and regulatory framework, innovation and a qualified workforce (Swiss Federal Council 2009). The financial market crisis also intensified the trend towards protectionist measures; such restrictions prove a hindrance to cross-border business (Swiss Federal Council 2009). Therefore, the priority is on strengthening competitiveness, improving the Swiss financial sector's entry to the most important markets abroad, safeguarding the stability of Swiss financial institutions, and increasing confidence in the financial center and its integrity (Swiss Federal Council 2009). In addition, the traditional strengths of the Swiss financial center (protection of assets through political stability, legal certainty, a strong currency, protection of privacy) are playing an increasingly marginal role, as the gap between Switzerland and other countries continues to narrow (Swiss Federal Council 2009). Furthermore, Switzerland has also come under increasing pressure from individual neighboring countries, the EU, the U.S., and international institutions to reform its banking secrecy laws (CIA 2012). In 2009, Swiss financial regulators ordered the country's largest bank to reveal at Washington's behest the names of U.S. account-holders suspected of using the bank to commit tax fraud. These steps will have a lasting impact on Switzerland's long history of bank secrecy (CIA 2012).

International cooperation: International cooperation needs to be stepped up in order to ensure effective regulation and better coordination of the various national supervisory authorities in times of crisis (Swiss Federal Council 2009). Thus, the existing cooperative arrangements with financial authorities in other countries need to be expanded for the largest Swiss banks and insurance companies and for crisis management in the event of future problems (OECD 2009b).

Political system: Based on the current political system, Switzerland's legislative process is traditionally quite slow and is characterized by multilateral compromise among the various interests. The advantage is continuity, predictability, and a well-balanced legal framework. Yet, the drawback is that Switzerland cannot align its conditions sufficiently, rapidly, and consistently with the international competitive situation (Swiss Federal Council 2009). In several cases, this has resulted in a loss of various trading activities and investment funds.

Bilateral agreement: Keeping step with the many decisions and reforms in the EU to preserve Switzerland's tried and true "bilateral approach" represents an additional challenge (Fuentes et al. 2011). Not an EU member, the Swiss government has to renegotiate its double taxation agreements with numerous countries, to incorporate the OECD standard, and it is working with Germany and the UK to resolve outstanding issues, particularly the possibility of imposing taxes on bank deposits held by foreigners.

Policy Implications

Unexpectedly, what started off as a sub-prime mortgage problem in the U.S. triggered a widespread global financial crisis. Even the relatively wealthy and advanced small European countries reported in this volume were not immune from the impact, because of their high reliance on export with small domestic markets.

The causes of this financial crisis are multifaceted. In addition to the much blamed high risk financial products, undisclosed conflicts of interest, failure of regulation and the credit rating agencies, the sovereignty debt problem broke out in the European Union region adds more complex dimensions to this crisis. The over liberation of banking industry, fragile financial system, and weak national governance surfaced all together at one time. It is a linking system breakdown that failed to withhold the impact of sudden financial shock.

Behind the statistics (such as percentage GDP growth drop and export volume decrease) are the hidden intangibles—the people, systems, governance, market dynamics, and regulation flaws that resulted in this global financial catastrophe. NIC research reported in this booklet covers human capital, market capital, process capital, and renewal capital encompassing key intangible elements described above. Our data analysis uncovered individual national intangible assets as well as country cluster comparisons and provide valuable information for the policy makers to look back the NIC before the crisis, observe the situation during the crisis, and study its progression afterward.

By investigating the economic development and NIC development spanning 2005–2010 at the same time, we have been able to connect the co-evolution of the tangibles and the intangibles for the four small European countries. Some implications can be drawn from our research findings as follows:

First, reducing government deficit through effective public spending and continuous structural reforms is the first priority in the wake of financial crisis. Common in most of the countries in the aftermath of this financial crisis is the buildup of government deficit due to the stimulus packages. Consolidation is to be continued in some countries, such as Belgium and The Netherlands. On the one hand, curbing public spending was advocated by reducing social benefits, cutting early retirement incentives, extending retirement age and so on; on the other hand, increasing revenues can be achieved through continuous structural reforms by broadening the tax base such as property tax and carbon tax, reforming health care system and pension system. In addition, our 3D NIC development trajectory unveils that government related issues are important impeding factors to GDP growth including convenience of establishing new firms, government efficiency, and transparency of government policy, summarized in Tables 3.3 and 3.4. The findings provide clear guidelines for the government to effectively implement coping measures for future economic development other than planned reforms.

Second, government's swift and focused intervention of large banks was critical for stabilizing the financial markets thus reduced the negative impact of the financial crisis. One of the key reasons for the relatively good recovery of these small European countries was the government's swift and focused intervention of large banks in trouble. All four countries have dominant banking conglomerates that are actively expanding their financial activities across national borders, especially in the central and eastern European countries that were seriously impacted by the financial crisis. Shortly after the banking crisis emerged, each individual government took swift and decisive actions to either nationalize the bank, such as Fortis in Belgium; or acquire distressed assets, such as UBS in Switzerland and KBC in Belgium to stabilize the financial market. With government capital support and guarantees, the financial markets were not disturbed too much to a detrimental level. The effects are manifested by their relatively fast recovery and Switzerland even reduced its government debt during the financial crisis.

Third, effectively assessing cross-border financial information through international cooperation facilitates the supervision of financial activities outside of the country. Due to the small domestic markets and the convenience of their geographical locations in Europe, these four countries have to and will continue their financial institution expansion to the central and eastern European countries. The need for intensified international cooperation to ensure effective regulation and to make the necessary improvements in coordinating the supervisory authorities in times of crisis was highlighted during this financial crisis. The expansion of pan-European banking supervision mechanisms proposed by Belgium and Switzerland will benefit most European countries if simultaneously strengthening existing venues of cooperation.

Fourth, high value-added products and services in a niche market can mitigate the external impact. Switzerland weathered this financial crisis the best among these four small European countries and was the first country to emerge from this global financial crisis in Europe (Doerig 2009). In addition, it was ranked number one in global competitiveness by the 2011–2012 World Economic Forum report, its GDP per capita (ppp) is consistently the highest among these four countries, and its national intellectual capital is ranked number two in our 48-country profile. In other words, Switzerland is strong in both the tangibles and intangibles. As reported in Chap. 2, one of the main reasons is its high value-added pharmaceutical and medical devices industries, which account for about 35 % of Swiss exports, and the product nature is not susceptible to external impact. On the contrary, Belgium has been losing its market share since 1995, as Belgian exporters do not specialize enough in differentiated high-value added products and suffer from eroding competitiveness in unit labor cost terms (IMF 2009).

Fifth, market diversification is important to reduce external impact for export-reliant countries. Another reason of Switzerland's fast recovery is its market diversification. As reported in Chap. 2, Switzerland also conducts a substantial share of foreign trade with emerging countries, particularly with China in addition to its 50 % of exports to the Euro area. During this financial crisis, China experienced virtually no slackening of growth and relatively stable export to China has helped Swiss recovery.

Sixth, national intellectual capital development goes together with the economic development and should be regarded as an enhancer of economic growth. From Fig. 3.7, it is very clear that high NIC explains high GDP. For the two higher GDP countries—Switzerland and The Netherlands, in almost every NIC graph we presented, Switzerland (except market capital) has the best result and The Netherlands has the second best result (except renewal capital) among the four countries, irrespective to during or after the financial crisis. The lowest GDP country—Belgium consistently has the lowest NIC result (except human capital) among the four countries. These findings provide the rationale for promoting intangible national intellectual capital, especially in the knowledge economy that intangible assets are becoming increasingly important.

Seventh, detecting early warnings and designing country-specific strategy facilitate a more focused NIC development. Even though these four countries have relative good performance in terms of GDP and NIC, our research still reveal early warnings. In our research, Austria has the greatest ranking drop in market capital (Fig. 3.17) and its short-term NIC (market capital and process capital) was declining most drastically among the four countries, starting from 2006. Even though the country recovered very well after the financial crisis, its international reserves (Appendix 7) is less than half that of Belgium in 2010 (US$8,091 million vs. US$16,161 million). Table 3.3 also indicates that market capital issues are Austria's important impeding factors to the targeted GDP growth. Belgium has the best human capital ranking (#8) among the four countries, yet Table 3.3 indicates that human capital issues turned out to be important impeding factors to the targeted GDP growth, especially after the financial crisis (such as employee training). R&D issues are also important impeding factors for Belgium, which rely heavily on the quality of human capital. The Netherlands has the best market capital ranking (#4) among the four countries, yet Table 3.3 indicates that market capital issues turned out to be its important impeding factors to the targeted GDP growth, especially before the financial crisis such as cross-border ventures and globalization. This finding somewhat agrees with the problems encountered by the Dutch financial institutions across its national borders. Switzerland used to have high quality manpower, yet Table 3.3 indicates that human capital issues turned out to be important impeding factors to the targeted GDP growth, both before and after the financial crisis such as skilled labor and public expenditure on education. This finding is also in agreement with Swiss Federal Council's (2009) warning that lacking of qualified workforce has become a barrier to cross-border market access.

The above findings highlight the areas each country can contemplate for mapping coping strategies. Since the intangible will be a key determinant of future competitiveness, identifying the focus of attention can more effectively allocate needed resources for improving the issues of concern.

Concluding Remarks and Emerging Insights

The global financial crisis was triggered in September 2008 by the U.S. sub-prime mortgage problems. As a result, a massive impact on the world economy has occurred, due to the drying-up of the interbank market, the tougher lending terms, higher borrowing costs, and tumbling stock markets. GDP has been shrunk worldwide as business and consumer confidence has dropped, leading to a marked decline in corporate investment, major destocking and a contraction in world trade. A sharp deterioration in labor markets followed, leading to hiking unemployment. The increasing international interdependencies, supervisory and regulatory systems that failed to adequately address the systemic risks, and the insufficient international banks transactions information disclosure all led to the outbreak of 2008 global financial crisis.

This global financial crisis came with an unexpected speed and negative effect, yet the governments of these four small European countries have navigated their countries through the crisis relatively well. The 2008 global financial crisis has provided an excellent opportunity for nations to assess the policy responses, to uncover the structural flaws, to discuss the options for restoring economic growth, and to re-construct a more resilient economy. Particularly, it became known that the existing crisis instruments in various countries are largely designed to deal with domestic failures and are no longer suitable for nowadays serious cross-border problems (Kellermann 2009), thus coping measures with international collaboration should be designed in the near future.

Apparently, the advent of the single financial market in Europe brings clear benefits especially for small economies like these four countries, yet it also poses additional supervisory challenges. The assignment of full supervisory responsibilities over credit rating agencies to the European Securities Markets Authority (ESMA) constitutes a good starting point for further centralization (Enoch et al. 2011). In addition, to counter the negative impact of red tape and burdensome regulatory systems on business development, Euro area could establish a business-friendly environment by increasing transparency, reducing the complexities of tax codes and compliance regulations, simplifying payment procedures through the use of e-government, and ensuring the stability of taxation legislation (Tajani 2011).

Presumably, national leaders should have learned some valuable lessons from this financial crisis and will have better foresight to evade from being trapped in similar situations again. However, such confidence comes from continuously responding to the social changes and reexamining the adequacy of national strategies, policies, and governance in coping with the increasingly interconnected and rapidly changing global economic environment.

As a recap, to counter the worsening economic conditions worldwide during the financial crisis, a total of US$2 trillion in stimulus packages (amounting to approximately 3 % of world gross domestic product) have been allocated (some of the packages include measures that extend into subsequent years), an amount that exceeds the call by the International Monetary Fund for fiscal stimulus totaling 2 % of global GDP (Nanto 2009).

This booklet briefly reports the main causes of why these four countries were dragged into the financial turmoil, how they came out of it, their positioning in the global NIC landscape, the NIC strength or weakness of each country, and the relationship between NIC and GDP.

As concerns over the aging population, shrinking workforce, and reduced productivity become more and more pressing in Europe, the health care, pension system, and labor regulation reforms should bring some positive effects in re-thinking these countries' future development. The challenges and policy implications presented above may provide some clues for building even more resilient economies for future sustainability.

At the completion of reporting the impact of the financial crisis on these four countries from national intellectual capital perspective, we have a strong feeling that national success is the capability that accumulates over time meticulously; it does not come quickly nor at will. National economic development is built upon well-coordinated tangible and intangible systems, including money, real assets, and human capital, market capital, process capital, and renewal capital systems described in this booklet. As the very origin of the financial crisis is people, systems, governance, market dynamics, and the global interdependence, they are also the keys to the economic recovery and national development in any place and country.

Appendix 1
Summary of the Main Stimulus Packages for Austria, Belgium, The Netherlands, and Switzerland

C. Y.-Y. Lin et al., *National Intellectual Capital and the Financial Crisis in Austria, Belgium, The Netherlands, and Switzerland*, SpringerBriefs in Economics,
DOI: 10.1007/978-1-4614-8021-1,

Country	Date	Amount	Item
Austria	2008	#1 US$127.6bn (€90bn) US$4.3bn (€3bn)	US$106.3bn (€75bn) guarantees, US$21.3bn (€15bn) for equity capital strengthening, 2009 tax reform, additional budget for R&D, family subsidies, and lower VAT for pharmaceuticals
	Dec. 2008	#2 US$1.4bn (€1bn)	US$67.8 mn (€50 mn) of micro-credits for small companies, and US$1.2bn (€875 mn) for public buildings, university buildings, and thermal retrofitting.
		#3 US$2.7bn (€2bn)	Including US$204.9 mn (€150 mn) for regional employment programs, US$300.5 mn (€220 mn) for expansion of short-time work scheme, US$95.6 mn (€70 mn) for mandatory and free kindergarten, US$1.2bn (€900 mn) for investments in rail and road infrastructure and US$61.5 mn (€45 mn) for a car scrapping scheme
	2009–2010	#4 Around 4.2 % of 2008 GDP	The stimulus package has preserved a cumulated 41,500 jobs that may otherwise had been lost, decreasing the rise in the rate of unemployment by 0.7 percentage points
Belgium	Dec. 2008	#5 US$273bn (€200bn)	Equivalent to 1.5 % of aggregated gross domestic product (GDP)
	Dec. 11, 2008	#6	The regional stimulus packages focus on ensuring the access to financing of corporations, in particular SMEs and start-ups, and on public investment. The package aims at: Providing support to corporations by improving their liquidity position, reducing the tax wedge on labor, and stimulating the residential construction market through a targeted and temporary VAT reduction; Supporting a better follow-up of dismissed workers due to restructuring, more forceful outplacement obligations, improved access to training and qualifications as well as better advice to job seekers; Ensuring the purchasing power of households by temporarily increasing unemployment benefits for temporary unemployed and additional subsidies for heating oil; Temporarily stepping up public investment, mainly in infrastructure

(continued)

(continued)

Country	Date	Amount	Item
Netherlands	Nov. 2008	#7 US$7.5bn (€6bn) US$25bn (€20bn) guarantee	The Dutch government nationalized two major banks ABN Amro and Fortis US$25bn (€20bn) was injected into Dutch money market to guarantee interbank transfers and thereby restore confidence of investors and consumers: 1. Aegon, an insurance company, received a sum of US$3.8bn (€3bn) 2. ING received US$12.7bn (€10bn) as booster funds. Holland economic stimulus package has also made provisions for foreign direct investments
	Nov. 2008	#8 US$10bn (€8bn)	The Dutch government approved an economic stimulus package worth up to US$10bn (€8bn) to help the country cope with the global financial crisis.
	Mar. 26, 2009	#9 US$7.9bn (€6bn)	The Dutch government proposed a new stimulus package of US$7.9bn (€6bn) (equivalent to about 1% of gross domestic product) for 2009 and 2010, to be spent over six years Dutch provinces and municipalities are to have an additional US$2bn (€1.5bn) to invest, including: Retraining programs would be made available and top priority would be given to preventing youth unemployment; Investment in sustainability, energy security, renewable energy, innovation, and schemes for scrapping old cars and for insulating homes; For infrastructure and construction, priorities were for road and waterway maintenance, improvement of school and hospital buildings or the construction of new ones; Promoting company liquidity, by abolishing the flight tax and raising the liquidity of companies connected with Schiphol Airport
Switzerland	Nov. 2008	#10 US$732mn (CHF890mn)	The government announced an economic stimulus package worth US$732 mn (CHF890 mn), including US$285 mn (CHF340 mn) on flood defense, natural disasters, and energy-efficiency projects Spending also included up to US$839mn (CHF1bn) on roads and railways and US$461 mn (CHF550 mn) as tax breaks to 650 firms for job creation programs

(continued)

(continued)

Country	Date	Amount	Item
	Feb. 11, 2009	#11 US$606.7mn (CHF700mn)	The Swiss government announced a second series of financial measures to stabilize the economy, especially directed at the transportation sector
	Jun. 2009	#12 US$690mn (CHF750mn)	The third stimulus package was aimed at "softening the consequences of the recession and encouraging a return to growth." About US$366 mn (CHF400 mn), was aimed at tackling unemployment The rest included support for innovative small- and medium-sized businesses, US$219 mn (CHF 200 mn) to cut the cost of personal health insurance, and US$137 mn (CHF150 mn) to reform Value Added Tax (VAT)

#1. Steger G (2009) Budgeting under and beyond the stimulus: Lessons learned. http://www.oecd.org/dataoecd/40/23/44308950.pdf.Accessed Nov 2009

#2. Meyer-Ohlendorf N, Görlach B, Umpfenbach K, Mehling M. (2009) *Economic Stimulus in Europe – Accelerating Progress towards Sustainable Development?* Ecologic Institute: Berlin. http://www.sd-network.eu/pdf/doc_prague/ESDN_Recovery_Report_020709_FINAL.pdf. Accessed June 2009

#3. Breuss F, Kaniovski S, Schratzenstaller M (2009) Macro-economic effects of the fiscal stimulus measures in Austria. *Austrian Economic Quarterly* (14.4) 205–216. http://fritz.breuss.wifo.ac.at/Breuss_Kaniovski_Schratzenstaller_Macro-economic_Effects_Fiscal_Stimulus_Austria_AEQ_4_2009.PDF

#4. OECD (2009) *Policy Responses to the Economic Crisis: Investing in innovation for long-term growth.* http://www.oecd.org/dataoecd/59/45/42983414.pdf. Accessed June 2009

#5. Economy Watch (2010a) Belgium economic stimulus package. http://www.economywatch.com/economic-stimulus-package/belgium.html. Accessed 30 June 2010

#6. European Commission (2009) Belgium: Macro fiscal assessment. http://ec.europa.eu/economy_finance/economic_governance/sgp/pdf/20_scps/2008-09/02_technical_assessment/be_2009-07-08_ta_en.pdf. Accessed 8 July 2009

#7. Economy Watch (2010b) Netherlands economic stimulus package. http://www.economywatch.com/economic-stimulus-package/netherlands.html. Accessed 30 June 2010

#8. CNN (2008) Dutch move on $10 billion rescue program. http://edition.cnn.com/2008/WORLD/europe/11/21/dutch.economy/index.html. Accessed 21 Nov 2008

#9. Zeldin W (2009) Netherlands: new stimulus package, Library of Congress. http://www.loc.gov/lawweb/servlet/lloc_news?disp3_l205401227_text. Accessed 17 April 2009

#10. Reuters (2008) Factbox – Europe's fiscal stimulus plans to tackle crisis. http://www.reuters.com/article/2008/12/08/eu-financial-stimulus-idUSL87090 20081208. Accessed 8 Dec 2008

#11. China View (2009) Switzerland announces new stimulus package to boost economy, Xinhua News Agency. http://news.xinhuanet.com/english/2009-02/12/content_10804018.htm. Accessed 11 Feb 2009

#12. Expatica (2009) Swiss government unveils new stimulus. http://www.expatica.com/ch/news/local_news/Swiss-government-unveils-new-stimulus-_53706.html. Accessed 18 June 2009

Appendix 2
Important Meetings Held by World Leaders to Address the 2008 Global Financial Crisis

Date	Place	Participants
June 18–19, 2012	Los Cabos, Mexico	G20
June 17, 2012	Los Cabos, Mexico	G7 finance ministers
March 1–2, 2012	Brussels	European council
January 30, 2012	Brussels	Informal meeting of members of the European council
December 8–9, 2011	Brussels	European council
November 12–13, 2011	Honolulu, USA	19th APEC economic leaders' meeting
November 3–4, 2011	Cannes, France	G20
October 23, 2011	Brussels	European council
September 10, 2011	Marseille	G8 Deauville partnership finance ministers
September 9–10, 2011	Marseille	G7 finance ministers and central bank governors
July 21, 2011	Brussels	Meeting of heads of state or government of the Euro area
June 23–24, 2011	Brussels	European council
March 24–25, 2011	Brussels	European council
March 17, 2011	Japan	G7 finance ministers telephone conference
March 11, 2011	Brussels	Extraordinary European council
February 4, 2011	Brussels	European council
December 16–17, 2010	Brussels	European council
November 21, 2010	Ireland	G7 finance ministers
November 13–14, 2010	Yokohama, Japan	18th APEC economic leaders' meeting
November 11–12, 2010	Seoul, Korea	G20
October 28–29, 2010	Brussels	European council
October 8, 2010	Washington DC	G7 finance ministers and central bank governors
September 16, 2010	Brussels	European council
June 26–27, 2010	Toronto, Canada	G20
June 17, 2010	Brussels	European council
March 25–26, 2010	Brussels	European council
February 11, 2010	Brussels	Informal meeting of heads of state or government of the European union

(continued)

C. Y.-Y. Lin et al., *National Intellectual Capital and the Financial Crisis in Austria, Belgium, The Netherlands, and Switzerland*, SpringerBriefs in Economics,
DOI: 10.1007/978-1-4614-8021-1, © The Author(s) 2014

(continued)

Date	Place	Participants
February 5–6, 2010	Iqaluit, Nunavut, Canada	G7 finance ministers and central bank governors
December 10–11, 2009	Brussels	European council
November 19, 2009	Brussels	Informal meeting of heads of state or government of the European union
November 14–15, 2009	Singapore	17th APEC economic leaders' meeting
October 29–30, 2009	Brussels	European council
October 3, 2009	Istanbul, Turkey	G7 finance ministers and central bank governors
September 24–25, 2009	Pittsburgh, USA	G20
September 17, 2009	Brussels	Informal meeting of heads of state or government of the European union
June 18–19, 2009	Brussels	European council
June 12–13, 2009	Lecce, Italy	G8 finance ministers
April 24, 2009	Washington DC	G7 finance ministers and central bank governors
April 2, 2009	G20 London Summit, United Kingdom	G20
March 19–20, 2009	Brussels	European council
February 2009	Rome	G7 finance ministers and central bank governors
December 11–12, 2008	Brussels	European council
November 2008	Peru	G20 APEC
November 22–23, 2008	Lima, Peru	16th APEC economic leaders' meeting
November 14–15, 2008	Washington D.C., USA	G7
October 15–16, 2008	Brussels	European council
October 10, 2008	Washington, DC	G7 finance ministers
September 1, 2008	Brussels	Extraordinary European council
July 7–9, 2008	Tokyo, Japan	34th G8 summit
June 19–20, 2008	Brussels	European council
June 13–14, 2008	Osaka	G8 finance ministers meeting
March 13–14, 2008	Brussels	European council
February 9, 2008	Tokyo	G7 finance ministers and central bank governors meeting

For further information:

http://g20mexico.org/en/g20/previous-leaders-summits

http://www.g8.utoronto.ca/finance/index.htm

http://video.consilium.europa.eu/ecofin/

http://www.european-council.europa.eu/council-meetings/conclusions

http://www.apec.org/

Appendix 3
Indicators in Each Type of Capital

Human capital index	Market capital index
1. Skilled labor*	1. Corporate tax*
2. Employee training*	2. Cross-border venture*
3. Literacy rate	3. Openness of culture*
4. Higher education enrollment	4. Globalization*
5. Pupil-teacher ratio	5. Transparency*
6. Internet subscribers	6. Image of country*
7. Public expenditure on education	7. Exports of goods
Process capital index	*Renewal capital index*
1. Business competition environment*	1. Business R&D spending
2. Government efficiency*	2. Basic research*
3. Intellectual property rights protection*	3. R&D spending/GDP
4. Capital availability*	4. R&D researchers
5. Computers in use per capita	5. Cooperation between universities and enterprises*
6. Convenience of establishing new firms*	6. Scientific articles
7. Mobile phone subscribers	1. Patents per capita (USPTO + EPO)

Remarks

1. Financial capital is the logarithm of GDP per capita adjusted by purchasing power parity.
2. Indicators marked with an asterisk are rated qualitatively using a scale of 1–10.
3. Indicators with objective numbers are transformed to 1–10 scores, by calculating the ratio to the highest number in that indicator and then multiply 10.
4. Readers can refer to the book *National Intellectual Capital: A Comparison of 40 Countries* for model validation details (www.nic40.org)

C. Y.-Y. Lin et al., *National Intellectual Capital and the Financial Crisis in Austria, Belgium, The Netherlands, and Switzerland*, SpringerBriefs in Economics,
DOI: 10.1007/978-1-4614-8021-1,

Appendix 4
Definition of the 29 Indicators

Indicators	Definition
Human Capital	
Skilled labor*	Whether skilled labor is readily available
Employee training*	Whether employee training is a high propriety in companies
Literacy rate	Adult (over 15 years) literacy rate as a percentage of population
Higher education enrollment	Percentage of population that has attained at least tertiary education
Pupil-teacher ratio	Ratio of teaching staff to students
Internet subscribers	Number of internet users per 1000 people
Public expenditure on education	Total public expenditure on education (percentage of GDP)
Market Capital	
Corporate tax encouragement*	Whether corporate taxes encourage entrepreneurial activity
Cross-border venture*	Whether international transactions can be freely negotiated with foreign partners
Openness to foreign culture*	Whether the national culture is open to foreign culture ideas
Attitudes toward globalization*	Whether attitudes toward globalization are generally positive in a given society
Transparency*	Whether transparency of government policy is satisfactory
Country image*	Whether the image abroad of a given country encourages business development
Exports of goods	Exports of goods (Percentage of GDP)
Process Capital	
Business competition environment*	Whether competition legislation is efficient in preventing unfair competition
Government efficiency*	Whether government bureaucracy hinders business activity
Intellectual property rights protection*	Whether intellectual property rights are adequately enforced
Capital availability*	Whether cost of capital encourages business development
Computers in use per capita	Number of computers per 1000 people

(continued)

C. Y.-Y. Lin et al., *National Intellectual Capital and the Financial Crisis in Austria, Belgium, The Netherlands, and Switzerland*, SpringerBriefs in Economics,
DOI: 10.1007/978-1-4614-8021-1,

(continued)

Indicators	Definition
Convenience of establishing new firms*	Whether creation of firms is supported by legislation
Mobile phone subscribers	Number of subscribers per 1000 inhabitants
Renewal Capital	
Business R&D spending	Business expenditure on R&D (per capita)
Basic research*	Whether basic research enhances long-term economic development
R&D spending/GDP	Total expenditure on R&D (percentage of GDP)
R&D researchers	Total R&D personnel nationwide per capita (Full-time work equivalent per 1000 people)
Cooperation between universities and enterprises*	Whether knowledge transfer is highly developed between universities and companies
Scientific articles	Scientific articles published by origin of author (per capita)
Patents per capita (USPTO + EPO)	USPTO and EPO total patents granted (per capita)
Financial Capital	
GDP per capita (PPP) (From IMF)	Gross domestic product based on purchasing power parity (PPP) per capita

Appendix 5
48 Countries by Cluster and by Continent

This booklet series covers a total of 48 countries in 11 country clusters. China, Brazil, and South Africa are grouped twice to maintain cluster completeness. China is in both Greater China region and BRICKS region, Brazil is in both BRICKS region and Latin American region, and South Africa is in both BRICKS region and in Cluster 5.

Eleven country clusters:

1. Portugal, Italy, Greece, Spain
2. Greater China region (China, Hong Kong, Singapore, Taiwan)
3. Brazil, Russia, India, China, Korea, South Africa (BRICKS)
4. Indonesia, Malaysia, The Philippines, Thailand
5. Israel, Jordan, Turkey, South Africa
6. Bulgaria, Czech Republic, Hungary, Romania, Poland
7. Austria, Belgium, The Netherlands, Switzerland
8. France, Germany, Ireland, United Kingdom
9. Argentina, Brazil, Chile, Colombia, Mexico, Venezuela
10. Australia, Canada, Japan, New Zealand, USA
11. Denmark, Finland, Iceland, Norway, Sweden

48 countries by continent:
Europe—24 countries
Nordic Europe—Denmark, Finland, Iceland, Norway, and Sweden
Western Europe—Austria, Belgium, France, Germany, Ireland, Netherlands, Switzerland, and UK
Southern Europe—Greece, Italy, Portugal, and Spain
Eastern Europe—Russia
East Central Europe—Bulgaria, Czech Republic, Hungary, Poland, Romania, and Turkey
Americas—8 countries
North America—Canada, USA
Latin America—Argentina, Brazil, Chile, Colombia, Mexico, and Venezuela

C. Y.-Y. Lin et al., *National Intellectual Capital and the Financial Crisis in Austria, Belgium, The Netherlands, and Switzerland*, SpringerBriefs in Economics,
DOI: 10.1007/978-1-4614-8021-1,

Australia—2 countries
Australia and New Zealand
Asia—13 countries
East Asia—China, Hong Kong, Japan, Korea, and Taiwan
West Asia—Israel, Jordan
Southeast Asia—Indonesia, Malaysia, Philippines, Singapore, and Thailand
South Asia—India
Africa—1 country
South Africa

Appendix 6
National Intellectual Capital Scores and Ranking for 48 Countries (2005–2010)

C. Y.-Y. Lin et al., *National Intellectual Capital and the Financial Crisis in Austria, Belgium, The Netherlands, and Switzerland*, SpringerBriefs in Economics,
DOI: 10.1007/978-1-4614-8021-1,

2005–2010	Human capital		Market capital		Process capital		Renewal capital		Financial capital		NIC	
Mean	6.420		5.409		5.345		3.658		9.115		29.946	
SD	1.217		1.085		1.454		2.056		0.690		5.840	
Country	Score	Ranking	Score	Ranking	Score	Ranking	Score	Ranking	Score	Ranking	Score	Ranking
Argentina	5.370	36	3.340	47	3.038	47	1.413	45	8.755	34	21.916	45
Australia	7.205	15	6.199	12	6.938	9	4.927	16	9.695	11	34.964	13
Austria	7.229	14	6.203	11	6.982	8	5.296	12	9.708	10	35.418	11
Belgium	7.666	8	5.519	23	5.924	21	4.706	17	9.635	14	33.450	19
Brazil	4.757	44	4.589	38	3.076	46	1.753	36	8.481	40	22.656	42
Bulgaria	5.493	34	4.929	31	4.054	36	1.589	41	8.646	37	24.710	35
Canada	7.855	6	6.137	13	6.464	15	5.064	14	9.710	9	35.229	12
Chile	5.414	35	6.663	5	5.163	28	1.710	37	8.784	32	27.734	30
China	4.942	39	5.184	28	3.746	40	2.099	33	7.967	44	23.938	40
Colombia	4.941	40	4.677	36	3.951	37	1.435	44	8.348	42	23.352	41
Czech Republic	5.995	30	5.720	18	5.378	25	2.905	24	9.271	27	29.269	25
Denmark	8.545	1	6.662	6	7.642	1	6.587	6	9.665	13	39.101	3
Finland	7.601	9	6.232	10	7.399	3	7.755	3	9.606	17	38.593	4
France	6.956	20	4.141	45	5.730	22	4.500	20	9.585	18	30.912	23
Germany	6.761	23	5.630	19	6.489	14	5.796	9	9.612	16	34.287	17
Greece	5.986	31	4.216	43	4.113	35	2.168	32	9.440	23	25.923	31
Hong Kong	6.564	25	8.090	2	7.209	5	3.277	23	9.794	4	34.934	14
Hungary	6.674	24	4.836	32	5.095	29	2.301	29	9.046	29	27.952	29
Iceland	8.357	3	5.614	21	6.561	12	5.931	8	9.713	8	36.154	8
India	3.926	48	5.620	20	3.556	42	1.954	34	7.285	48	22.340	44
Indonesia	4.062	47	4.832	33	3.257	44	1.519	42	7.594	46	21.263	47
Ireland	7.145	16	6.816	3	6.711	11	4.101	21	9.768	5	34.541	16
Israel	8.040	4	5.954	16	6.454	17	7.091	4	9.414	24	36.953	6

(continued)

(continued)

2005–2010	Human capital		Market capital		Process capital		Renewal capital		Financial capital		NIC	
Mean	6.420		5.409		5.345		3.658		9.115		29.946	
SD	1.217		1.085		1.454		2.056		0.690		5.840	
Country	Score	Ranking	Score	Ranking	Score	Ranking	Score	Ranking	Score	Ranking	Score	Ranking
Italy	6.471	28	4.155	44	5.184	27	2.745	26	9.479	22	28.035	28
Japan	7.581	10	4.820	34	6.209	18	6.473	7	9.576	19	34.659	15
Jordan	5.345	37	5.341	26	4.411	32	2.212	30	7.865	45	25.174	33
Korea	6.964	19	5.123	29	5.282	26	4.595	19	9.383	25	31.348	22
Malaysia	6.538	26	6.410	9	5.567	23	2.186	31	8.740	35	29.442	24
Mexico	4.871	42	4.491	39	3.226	45	1.237	48	8.781	33	22.606	43
Netherlands	7.312	12	6.761	4	6.879	10	5.163	13	9.739	7	35.855	10
New Zealand	7.123	18	5.999	15	6.460	16	3.701	22	9.380	26	32.662	21
Norway	7.936	5	6.055	14	7.008	7	4.961	15	9.987	1	35.947	9
Philippines	4.772	43	4.464	40	3.317	43	1.268	47	7.481	47	21.302	46
Poland	6.393	29	4.246	41	3.895	38	1.819	35	8.945	30	25.299	32
Portugal	6.882	22	4.801	35	5.470	24	2.467	27	9.224	28	28.844	26
Romania	5.829	32	4.219	42	3.806	39	1.685	38	8.594	39	24.133	39
Russia	5.530	33	3.860	46	3.588	41	2.349	28	8.822	31	24.150	38
Singapore	7.144	17	8.306	1	7.506	2	5.416	11	9.961	2	38.334	5
South Africa	4.708	45	4.976	30	4.472	31	1.677	39	8.472	41	24.306	37
Spain	6.524	27	4.649	37	5.033	30	2.787	25	9.484	21	28.476	27
Sweden	8.385	2	6.563	7	7.174	6	7.780	2	9.673	12	39.575	1
Switzerland	7.575	11	6.481	8	7.374	4	7.988	1	9.753	6	39.172	2
Taiwan	7.244	13	5.823	17	6.026	20	5.425	10	9.526	20	34.044	18
Thailand	5.310	38	5.524	22	4.365	33	1.436	43	8.304	43	24.938	34
Turkey	4.703	46	5.227	27	4.167	34	1.666	40	8.690	36	24.453	36
United Kingdom	6.939	21	5.440	24	6.090	19	4.697	18	9.626	15	32.793	20
USA	7.695	7	5.348	25	6.558	13	6.715	5	9.886	3	36.202	7
Venezuela	4.884	41	2.761	48	2.545	48	1.277	46	8.625	38	20.092	48

Appendix 7
Country Profile: Additional Statistics

1. International reserves in millions of US$

Country	2005	2006	2007	2008	2009	2010
Austria	8,138	7,605	7,519	10,955	6,493	8,091
Belgium	9,632	8,958	8,683	10,703	9,537	16,161
Netherlands	10,409	8,858	10,415	11,692	11,058	18,692
Switzerland	55,021	35,460	37,918	47,113	50,052	124,715

Source: Global Finance http://www.gfmag.com/

2. GDP per capita—PPP_ Current international dollar

Country	2005	2006	2007	2008	2009	2010
Austria	33,897	36,074	38,368	39,889	38,567	39,634
Belgium	32,100	33,799	35,490	36,248	35,337	36,100
Netherlands	35,021	37,330	39,847	41,323	39,860	40,765
Switzerland	35,816	38,085	40,273	41,405	40,484	41,663

Source: World Economic Outlook Database http://www.imf.org/external/ns/cs.aspx?id=28

3. GDP (PPP)—share of world total_%

Country	2005	2006	2007	2008	2009	2010
Austria	0.49	0.48	0.48	0.48	0.46	0.45
Belgium	0.60	0.58	0.57	0.56	0.55	0.53
Netherlands	1.01	0.99	0.98	0.97	0.95	0.92
Switzerland	0.47	0.46	0.46	0.45	0.45	0.44

Source: World Economic Outlook Database http://www.imf.org/external/ns/cs.aspx?id=28

C. Y.-Y. Lin et al., *National Intellectual Capital and the Financial Crisis in Austria, Belgium, The Netherlands, and Switzerland*, SpringerBriefs in Economics, DOI: 10.1007/978-1-4614-8021-1, © The Author(s) 2014

4. **Gross domestic expenditure on R&D as a % of GDP**

Country	2005	2006	2007	2008	2009	2010
Austria	2.26	2.36	2.45	2.56	2.67	2.75
Belgium	1.85	1.82	1.83	1.87	1.92	1.96
Netherlands	1.72	1.78	1.73	1.7	1.71	1.84
Switzerland	2.57	2.93	2.9	2.9	2.9	3

Source: IMD World Competitiveness Yearbook 2006-2011

5. **Household saving rates_ % of disposable household income**

Country	2005	2006	2007	2008	2009	2010
Austria	9.7	10.4	11.7	11.5	10.7	8.3
Belgium	10.1	10.8	11.4	11.7	13.7	11.2
Netherlands	6.4	6.1	6.9	5.9	6.4	3.9
Switzerland	10.1	11.4	12.6	11.7	12.0	10.7

Source: Global Finance http://www.gfmag.com/

Glossary

AFM Authority for Financial Markets in the Netherlands

APEC Asia-Pacific Economic Cooperation

Basel III Basel III is a global regulatory standard on bank capital adequacy, stress testing, and market liquidity risk agreed upon by the members of the Basel Committee on Banking Supervision in 2010–11, and scheduled to be introduced from 2013 until 2018. The third installment of the Basel Accords was developed in response to the deficiencies in financial regulation revealed by the 2008 financial crisis. Basel III strengthens bank capital requirements and introduces new regulatory requirements on bank liquidity and bank leverage. Basel III requires banks to hold 4.5 % of common equity (up from 2 % in Basel II) and 6 % of Tier I capital (up from 4 % in Basel II) of risk-weighted assets

BRIC Brazil, Russia, India, and China

BRICKS Brazil, Russia, India, China, Korea, and South Africa

CEE Central and east Europe

GHG Greenhouse gas

CPI Consumer price inflation

DNB De Nederlandsche Bank (Dutch National Bank) in the Netherlands

ECB European Central Bank

EFSF European Financial Stability Facility

EIB European Investment Bank

EIF European Investment Fund

EIU Economist Intelligence Unit

EPO European Patent Office

ESM European Stabilization Mechanism

C. Y.-Y. Lin et al., *National Intellectual Capital and the Financial Crisis in Austria, Belgium, The Netherlands, and Switzerland*, SpringerBriefs in Economics,
DOI: 10.1007/978-1-4614-8021-1, © The Author(s) 2014

ESMA European Securities Markets Authority

EU European Union

European Council One of the EU's regulatory bodies

FDI Foreign direct investment

FMA Austrian Financial Market Authority

GCI GCI Global Competitiveness Index (published by World Economic Forum)

GDP Gross domestic product

GDP per capita (ppp) Gross domestic product per capita adjusted by purchasing power parity

IMD International Institute for Management Development

IMF International Monetary Fund

HC Human capital

Long-term NIC Long-term oriented national intellectual capital, represented by human capital and renewal capital

MC Market capital

NIC National intellectual capital

OECD Organization for Economic Cooperation and Development

ONB Austrian National Bank (Oesterreichische National Bank)

PC Process capital

ppp Purchasing power parity

R&D Research and development

RC Renewal capital

SD Standard Deviation

Short-term NIC Short-term oriented national intellectual capital, represented by market capital and process capital

SMEs Small- and Medium-Sized Enterprises

SNB Swiss National Bank

Three time periods For the convenience of comparing ranking changes, the six years data were separated into three time periods, namely 2005-2006, 2007-2008, and 2009-2010. Two years each represents "before, during, and after" the 2008 global financial crisis. Even though Euro zone is still in sovereign debt trouble as of mid-2012, the time partition is based on the financial crisis progression in the epicenter. The signs of financial trouble appeared in 2007 and the crisis was declared over in the third quarter of 2009

UBS The largest bank in Switzerland

USPTO United States Patent and Trademark Office

VAT Value-added tax

References

Austrian Federal Economic Chamber (2011) This is Austria: location attractiveness for business and work, Austrian federal economic chamber, economic policy department. http://wko.at/wp

Beetsma R, Gradus R (2010) Filling the sustainability gap after the crisis: the case of the Netherlands, CESifo DICE report. http://www.cesifo-group.de/portal/pls/portal/docs/1/1192834.PDF

Breuss F, Kaniovski S, Schratzenstaller M (2009) Macro-economic effects of the fiscal stimulus measures in Austria, WIFO (Austrian Institute of Economic Research) study commissioned by the Federal ministry of economics, families and youth. http://fritz.breuss.wifo.ac.at/Breuss_Kaniovski_Schratzenstaller_Macro-economic_Effects_Fiscal_Stimulus_Austria_AEQ_4_2009.PDF

Bryant L (2011) Growth expected to slow in world's largest economies, voice of America news. http://www.voanews.com/english/news/europe/OECD–Economic-Slowdown-Likely-to-Continue-129458543.html. Accessed 8 Sept 2011

Central Intelligence Agency (CIA) (2012) The world factbook, U.S.A.Central Intelligence Agency. https://www.cia.gov/library/publications/the-world-factbook/index.html

CPB Netherlands Bureau for economic policy analysis (2011) Dutch economy in recession, prospects for 2012 depend on Eurozone crisis. http://www.cpb.nl/en/pressrelease/3211184/dutch-economy-recession-prospects-2012-depend-eurozone-crisis. Dec 13

CPB Netherlands Bureau for economic policy analysis (2012) Macro economic outlook (MEV) 2013. http://www.cpb.nl/en/publication/macro-economic-outlook-2013. Accessed 18 Sept 2012

Doerig HU (2009) In a better position than before the crisis: the swiss financial market has 'aaa' opportunities for the future, credit suisse group. https://www.credit-suisse.com/news/doc/speech_doerig_nzz_en.pdf. Accessed 11 Sept 2009

Dutch News (2011) Dutch economy virtually halted, recession in 2011 second-half, Dutch News. http://www.dutchnews.nl/news/archives/2011/12/dutch_economy_virtually_halted.php. Accessed 9 Dec 2011

Economist Intelligence Unit (EIU) (2010) Netherlands: financial services report, economist intelligence unit. http://www.eiu.com/index.asp?layout=ib3Article&article_id=737549058&pubtypeid=1132462498&category_id=775133077&country_id=1400000140&page_title=Forecast&rf=0. Accessed 22 Oct 2010

Edvinsson L, Malone MS (1997) *Intellectual Capital: Realizing your company's true value by finding its hidden brainpower*. HarperBusiness, New York

Enoch C, Moore M, Zhou J (2011) Financial system stability assessment—Netherlands, international monetary fund, monetary and capital markets and European departments. http://www.imf.org/external/pubs/ft/scr/2011/cr11144.pdf

Europa (2008). The Commission launches a major recovery plan for growth and jobs, to boost demand and restore confidence in the european economy. http://europa.eu/rapid/pressReleasesAction.do?reference=IP/08/

C. Y.-Y. Lin et al., *National Intellectual Capital and the Financial Crisis in Austria, Belgium, The Netherlands, and Switzerland*, SpringerBriefs in Economics, DOI: 10.1007/978-1-4614-8021-1, © The Author(s) 2014

1771&format=HTML&aged=0&language=EN&guiLanguage=en. Accessed 26 Nov 2008

Fathallah M (2010) Crisis country case study—Belgium, international social security association, Geneva. http://www.issa.int/

Federal Planning Bureau (2011) What has been the damage of the financial crisis to Belgian GDP? An assessment based on the FPB's medium-term outlook, federal planning Bureau, economic analysis and forecast, working paper 8–11. http://www.plan.be/admin/uploaded/201106221430150.wp201108.pdf. Accessed June 2011

Focus (2012) Switzerland: economic outlook, news and data, *Focus Economics*. http://www.focus-economics.com/en/economy/outlook/Switzerland

Fuentes A, Ramskogler P, Silgner MA (2011) The Swiss economy's resilience to crisis and its lessons for Austria, monetary policy & the economy Q2/11, oesterreichische nationalbank (OeNB). http://www.oenb.at/en/img/mop_2011_q2_analyse04_fuentes_tcm16-235937.pdf

Global Finance (2012) Belgium country report. http://www.gfmag.com/gdp-data-country-reports/318-belgium-gdp-country-report.html#axzz2Grvaavdv

Government of the Netherlands (n.d.) how did the Netherlands hand the credit crisis, Ministry of finance, government of the Netherlands. http://www.government.nl/issues/financial-policy/how-did-the-netherlands-hande-the-credit-crisis

Gurria A (2011a) Overview of the economic survey of Austria 2011, OECD. http://www.oecd.org/document/37/0,3746,en_2649_33733_48300453_1_1_1_1,00.html

Gurria A (2011b) Launch of the OECD economic survey of Austria 2011, OECD. http://www.oecd.org/document/20/0,3746,en_21571361_44315115_48373652_1_1_1_1,00.html

Gurria A (2011c) Overview of the economic survey of Belgium 2011, OECD. http://www.oecd.org/document/15/0,3746,en_2649_33733_48315471_1_1_1_1,00.html

Heritage Foundation (2011) Economic freedom, heritage foundation. http://www.heritage.org

Heritage Foundation (2012) Economic freedom, heritage foundation. http://www.heritage.org

IHS Global Insight (2012) Belgium economy expands 1.9% in 2011 but sinks into recession in Q4, IHS Global Insight. http://www.ihs.com/products/global-insight/industry-economic-report.aspx?id=1065932255. Accessed 2 Feb 2012

International Monetary Fund (IMF) (2009) Belgium: 2008 Article IV Consultation—staff report; staff supplement; and public information notice on the executive board discussion, IMF Country Report No. 09/87. http://www.imf.org/external/pubs/ft/scr/2009/cr0987.pdf. Accessed March 2009

Kehoe T (2010) The current financial crisis in Spain: what should we learn from the great depressions of the twentieth century? University of Minnesota and federal reserve bank of Minneapolis, 18th Barcelona Lecture, Barcelona G.S.E. and Banc Sabadell, Feb 2010

Kellermann J (2009) The financial crisis in the Netherlands: Measures taken and lessons learned, Seminar: A New World for Financial Industry? A comparative approach, Brussels. http://www.dnb.nl/binaries/The%20Financial%20Crisis%20in%20the%20Netherlands_tcm46-224708.pdf. Accessed 19 Nov 2009

Kratky C (2012) Ambitious Austria, innovation America. http://www.innovationamerica.us/index.php/innovation-daily/19255-ambitious-austria-public-service

Lachman D (2013) No easing in the European crisis, the online magazine of the American enterprise institute. www.american.com/archive/2013/january/no-easing-in-the-european-crisis. Accessed 2 Jan 2013

Lin CYY, Edvinsson L (2011) *National Intellectual Capital: A comparison of 40 countries*. Springer Publishing Co., New York

Market Research (2012) Belgium business forecast report Q1 2013, business monitor international. http://www.marketresearch.com/Business-Monitor-International-v304/Belgium-Business-Forecast-Q1-7195236/. Accessed 13 Nov 2012

Masselink M, Noord P (2009) The global financial crisis and its effects on the Netherlands, Economic analysis from the European commission's directorate-general for economic and financial affairs. *ECFIN Country Focus, 6(10)*, 1-7. ISSN 1725-8375. http://ec.europa.eu/economy_finance/publications/publication16339_en.pdf. Accessed 12 April 2009

Meel F (2009) EU27 country reports—Belgium, EMF HYPOSTAT. http://www.ecbc.eu/uploads/attachements/100/65/Belgium.pdf

Meier S (2012) Swiss outlook at risk after surprise GDP drop: Economy, Bloomberg. http://www.bloomberg.com/news/2012-09-04/swiss-economy-unexpectedly-shrank-in-second-quarter-on-exports.html. Accessed 4 Sept 2012

Mendonça JR (2010) The impact of the international financial crisis on Brazil. http://www.realinstitutoelcano.org/wps/portal/rielcano_eng/Content?WCM_GLOBAL_CONTEXT=/elcano/elcano_in/zonas_in/international+economy/ari38-2010

Moloney N (2010) EU financial market regulation after the global financial crisis: "More Europe" or more risks? Common Market Law Rev 47:1317–1383

Nanto DK (2009) The global financial crisis: analysis and policy implications. *CRS Report for Congress, Congressional Research Service 7-5700, RL34742*, 2 Oct, 2009)

Newsweek (2008) The Swiss way to beat a crisis, newsweek magazine. http://www.thedailybeast.com/newsweek/2008/12/06/the-swiss-way-to-beat-a-crisis.html. Accessed 5 Dec 2008

OECD (2009a) Economic survey of Austria 2009: facing the financial crisis, OECD. http://www.oecd.org/document/16/0,3746,en_2649_34111_43150160_1_1_1_1,00.html

OECD (2009b) Economic survey of Switzerland 2009, OECD. http://www.oecd.org/document/30/0,3343,en_2649_33733_44315358_1_1_1_1,00.html

OECD (2010) OECD Economic surveys: Netherlands 2010, OECD

OECD (2011a) Country notes—Belgium, restoring public finances, OECD. http://www.oecd.org/dataoecd/29/27/47840665.pdf

OECD (2011b) Country notes—Netherlands, restoring public finances, OECD. http://www.oecd.org/dataoecd/36/15/47860186.pdf

OECD (2011c) Country notes—Switzerland, restoring public finances, OECD. http://www.oecd.org/dataoecd/37/26/47860777.pdf

OECD (June 2012) OECD economic surveys: Netherlands June 2012, OECD. http://www.oecd.org/eco/50550641.pdf

ONB (Oesterreichische National Bank) (June 2012) Economic outlook for Austria from 2012 to 2014, ONB, economic analysis and research department, economic analysis division. http://www.oenb.at/en/img/prognose_mop_2_12_tcm16-248405.pdf

Palkamo A (2011) WEF ranks Finland as the fourth most competitive nation. *Tekes*. http://www.tekes.fi/en/community/News/482/News/1344?name=WEF+ranks+Finland+as+the+fourth+most+competitive+nation. Accessed 9 Aug 2011

QFinance (n.d.a) The Netherlands—Economy, QFinance. http://www.qfinance.com/country-profiles/the-netherlands

QFinance (n.d.b) Switzerland—Economy, QFinance. http://www.qfinance.com/country-profiles/switzerland

Rabobank (2012) Outlook 2012: how resilient is the economy? Rabobank, the Netherlands. http://www.rabobank.com/content/images/Outlook2012EN_tcm43-153694.pdf

Ragacs C, Vondra K (2009) Deep recession in Austria—stabilization expected at year-end: economic outlook for Austria from 2009 to 2011 (June 2009), Monetary Policy & The Economy Q2/2009. http://www.oenb.at/en/img/mop_2009_q2_analyses01_tcm16-141270.pdf

Reavis C (2009) The global financial crisis of 2008–2009: The role of greed, fear and oligarchs, MIT Sloan Management Case #09-093, published 2009.07.22

Reinhart CM, Rogoff KS (2009) *This Time is Different: Eight centuries of financial folly*. Princeton University Press, Princeton. ISBN 9780691142166

Reiss L, Kohler-Toglhofer W (n.d.) Implications of the crisis for public finances: the case of Austria, österreichische nationalbank. http://www.bancaditalia.it/studiricerche/convegni/atti/FiscalPolicy/Session4/Reiss_Koehler-Toeglhofer.pdf

Schwab K (ed) (2011) The global competitiveness report 2011–2012. World Economic Forum, Geneva

Seefeld M (2012) Prospects for the solar future Belgium II—interview with Edwin Koot, solar efficiency for future. http://www.solar-efficiency-for-future.org/articles/prospects-for-the-solar-future-belgium-12-interview-with-edwin-koot/. Accessed 19 March 2012

Swiss Federal Council (2009) Strategic directions for Switzerland's financial market policy: Report in response to the Graber postulate (09.3209), Accessed 16 Dec 2009

Tajani A (2011) Strengthening competitiveness, Europa speech, Oct. 14, 2011. http://europa.eu/rapid/press-release_SPEECH-11-669_en.htm?locale=en

Tanuro D (2008) Understanding the Belgian crisis, international viewpoint. http://www.internationalviewpoint.org/spip.php?article1426. Accessed Feb 2008

U.S. Department of State (2011) Background note: Austria, Bureau of European and Eurasian affairs, U.S. department of state: diplomacy in action. http://www.state.gov/r/pa/ei/bgn/3165.htm. Accessed 9 Dec 2011

U.S. Department of State (2012a) Background note: Belgium, Bureau of European and Eurasian affairs, U.S. department of state: diplomacy in action. http://www.state.gov/r/pa/ei/bgn/2874.htm. Accessed 22 March 2012

U.S. Department of State (2012b) Background Note: the Netherlands, Bureau of European and Eurasian affairs, U.S. department of state: diplomacy in action. http://www.state.gov/r/pa/ei/bgn/3204.htm. Accessed 22 March 2012

U.S. Department of State (2012c) Background note: Switzerland, Bureau of European and Eurasian affairs, U.S. department of state: diplomacy in action. http://www.state.gov/r/pa/ei/bgn/3431.htm. Accessed 23 Feb 2012

Van de Velde A (2011) Less government, more growth? Belgium get ahead, CNBC. http://www.cnbc.com/id/44449759/Less_Government_More_Growth_Belgium_Gets_Ahead. Accessed 9 Sept 2011

Author Index

C. Y.-Y. Lin et al., *National Intellectual Capital and the Financial Crisis in Austria, Belgium, The Netherlands, and Switzerland*, SpringerBriefs in Economics, DOI: 10.1007/978-1-4614-8021-1, © The Author(s) 2014

Subject Index

C. Y.-Y. Lin et al., *National Intellectual Capital and the Financial Crisis in Austria, Belgium, The Netherlands, and Switzerland*, SpringerBriefs in Economics,
DOI: 10.1007/978-1-4614-8021-1,

MIX
Papier aus verantwortungsvollen Quellen
Paper from responsible sources
FSC® C105338

If you have any concerns about our products,
you can contact us on
ProductSafety@springernature.com

In case Publisher is established outside the EU,
the EU authorized representative is:
Springer Nature Customer Service Center GmbH
Europaplatz 3, 69115 Heidelberg, Germany

Printed by Libri Plureos GmbH
in Hamburg, Germany